BOOSTING
ACHIEVEMENT

REACHING STUDENTS *with*
INTERRUPTED *or* MINIMAL EDUCATION

CAROL SALVA

with ANNA MATIS

Published by Seidlitz Education
P.O. Box 166827
Irving, TX 75016
www.seidlitzeducation.com

For related titles and support materials visit www.seidlitzeducation.com.

4.21

TABLE OF CONTENTS

FOREWORD 2

INTRODUCTION 6

PART I: WORKING WITH STUDENTS WHO ARE SIFE 12

Who are SIFE/Unschooled/Under-schooled Students? 12

What Do I Need to Know About Working with SIFE? 16

Getting Started 22

PART II: UNDERSTANDING GRIT & GROWTH MINDSET 32

Grit 32

Growth Mindset 35

Benefits of Hosting an International Student 38

Global Learning & Breaking International Barriers 40

Social Contract 45

PART III: ACCELERATING LANGUAGE DEVELOPMENT 48

Second Language Acquisition Basics 49

Content vs. ESL Teacher 57

Assessment 62

PART IV: IMPLEMENTING A PRACTICAL
APPROACH TO INSTRUCTION 64

Listening and Speaking 65

    QSSSA 66

    Roving Paragraph Frames 67

Acquiring Literacy 72

    Reading 76

    Language Experience Approach 82

Writing 85

    Scaffolded Paragraph Frames 88

    Writing in Content Areas 90

RESOURCES & COMMUNITY PARTNERS 92

Resources for Continued Growth

Community Partners

Online Resources

SOURCES 96

FOREWORD

I am searching for that which every person seeks - peace and rest.
— Dante Alighieri

MY FAMILY WERE AMONG THE LAST WAVE OF BOAT REFUGEES who fled South Vietnam after its fall in 1975. My siblings and I weren't permitted to attend quality schools there because our family aided the American troops during the war. Faced with a future filled with doors slammed shut, my mother, along with other families who were choked by similar restrictions, decided to illegally charter a boat to escape in 1986. The odds of surviving the voyage were stacked in favor of the sea. Under the cover of darkness, we fled and floated towards Malaysia. One day after the fuel had run out and with only one day left until the fresh water and food would do the same, a Malaysian Navy boat rescued us and eventually resettled our family in a Filipino camp for Vietnamese migrants.

We spent 18 months at the refugee camp in the Philippines awaiting our permanent relocation to the United States. Wanting to educate the children in the refugee camps, humanitarian organizations eventually opened up schools. First born sons can be burdened with pressures to protect and provide. This burden forced my brother to drop out of high school and do odd handyman jobs to support his family. But my second oldest brother enrolled in middle school while my sister joined the elementary school. I was just old enough to enroll in the kindergarten when we were granted entry into the United States.

We were grateful for the makeshift refugee schools because they provided some semblance of a normal life for us and the other refugee children. But because of the conditions at the camp and the lack of resources, my brothers and sister experienced some interrupted formal education.

Thirty years later, my story is repeated in the on-going, living nightmares that haunt today's refugees. Recent wars and the destabilization of some countries in the Middle East, parts of Africa, regions in Asia, and segments of Latin America have produced a global humanitarian crisis. American schools are seeing a rise in Students with Interrupted Formal Education (SIFE) from people who, like my family, were forced to renounce their homelands in exchange for safety. How do teachers serve children who have been on the road running from the grip of a tyrannical government, or teach students who must migrate with their families from farm to farm to harvest crops?

We might receive training on how to work with English learners (ELs), but these strategies and approaches often rely on ELs having formal education in their home countries and established literacy skills in their home languages. Educators have to use a different approach to serving those students who have limited or no previous access to formal education. Sadly, little, if any, of our training or professional development addresses ways to serve this specific demographic. Carol Salva and Anna Matis have responded with this book - published at a time when schools and teachers need their advice more than ever.

I first met Carol on social media where we were both interested in developing digital EL resources. After ten years of teaching and reading books on teaching practices, I decided to share my most effective language development strategies on my blog, EmpoweringELLs.com. Carol retweeted my articles and was a valuable contributor on the weekly #ellchat. When I co-founded an online book club devoted to reading books about EL instruction (#ellchat_bkclub) with Katie Toppel (@Toppel_ELD), she joined the book club and contributed to our collective growth by posting pictures and videos of her work with children and sharing links to articles with concrete, implementable ideas.

Upon seeing how much my own craft was improving from connecting with other educators on Twitter, I decided to start a virtual conference for English language teachers to connect with innovative educators who find ways for ELs to succeed. I needed someone who would enthusiastically partner with me to take this idea from dream into reality - albeit a virtual one. Carol, of course, agreed to shepherd this project so that teachers don't have to feel like they're alone in advocating for ELs. Her first contribution - creating our hashtag: #VirtuEL17.

Carol's excitement, commitment, and expertise in this field, however, can't be contained in just 140 characters, which is why I'm so enthusiastic about recommending the book she has co-authored with writer and ESL educational consultant, Anna Matis.

In *Boosting Achievement: Reaching Students with Interrupted or Minimal Education*, Carol uses her teaching experience and specialty knowledge of language development to distill seminal research on SIFE into a teacher-friendly framework.

Suggesting that content instruction should not be the only educational priority, Carol recommends making space for students to develop something more important: a growth mindset. After all, experiences for students who are SIFE will most likely be new, anxiety-producing, and challenging. This whirling storm of confusion comes from having to learn foreign cultural practices, a process made increasingly more difficult by not knowing English. A growth mindset will remind students who are SIFE to return to the effective strategies that helped them acquire language and learn American cultural expectations. Through this process, they'll learn to address what they can control, and gracefully release things they can't.

We all know that our students - SIFE or not - will face challenges for the rest of their lives. I'm certain that Carol's advice to teach them to be the masters of their inner world, when their outer world is crumbling, will be useful more often than any content taught in an era of teaching to pass standardized tests.

In addition to these essential emotional skills, Salva and Matis focus on providing teachers with specific literacy strategies that scaffold content and develop language skills. No wonder they are highly sought after consultants, and their presentations at conferences are standing-room only.

These strategies can create a word-rich environment where students use language to solve problems, ask questions, and defend opinions. I am impressed by all the ways Carol holds high expectations for SIFE and am inspired by their authentic learning experiences. Check out her lesson on page 44 that incorporates a chef and owner of a high-end restaurant as an example of authentic learning.

Another of my favorite strategies in the book is the Structured Conversation, also known as Question, Signal, Stem, Share, Assess (QSSSA), in Part IV. Many SIFE come from countries with an orally-rich tradition where speaking and socializing are the main currency of communication. Because they're used to talking to create meaning and establish order, the social aspect of QSSSA is more approachable, and can be used across content areas and grade levels.

Even at their young ages, many SIFE come to America with enough pain to fill a lifetime of sadness and despair. Their bodies might be here, but their hearts and prayers remain with those whom they've left behind. They are grateful for this new home free of persecution, without a tightening noose around their lives, but they ache for their real homes and for the people they couldn't bring along.

Our field is brimming with books on instructing ELs, but few speak directly to SIFE. I foresee districts directing teachers to this book as a must-read to serve a population we must not forget. It will become a classic in the field, and one I will run to when a student who is SIFE joins my school.

Together with Salva and Matis, we can honor the bravery and sacrifice of learners who are SIFE by making our classrooms places where we shelter them from the rain of insults, where we open our hearts so that they can lower their walls, where hope floats, and where for the first time in a long time, they're allowed to be children who are finally granted what we all seek: peace and rest.

Tan Huynh

EmpoweringELLs.com
Co-founder of
#ellchat_bkclub and #VirtuEL17

The classroom kept turning into chaos.

Fights would break out right in front of me, even with two adults in the room. This was the scene that unfolded during my weekly visits to a school that I supported as an ESL Teacher on Special Assignment. I was visiting Ms. Ferguson's room weekly because the campus was requesting assistance and I supported secondary ESL. One visit a week was not nearly enough. We all knew this campus needed another teacher, and evidently, frequent visits. Ms. Ferguson taught over 30 newcomers, many of whom were SIFE (Students with Interrupted Formal Education), and the population continued to grow. I felt like I wasn't helping her at all. Despite our combined decades of classroom management and sheltered instruction strategies under our belts, my efforts felt inadequate. This was a situation that neither of us had ever experienced. Irma Batra, another ESL teacher, also worked with the students to help them gain literacy, but again, resources were limited.

These middle school students were refugees, a majority of whom were non-English speakers. Many were coming from refugee camps where they had spent several years. Some of these students had been born in the camps. Their families were resettled here from different African countries so there was no common language.

For me, it was such a culture shock to be in the room with all of them. Many of the students had a halting way of speaking that was normal for them, but sometimes seemed aggressive and threatening. Snatching and grabbing items from each other was a constant issue. These habits were likely due to the fact that many were coming from a lifestyle where resources were extremely scarce. Pushing and shoving versus waiting in a line was a common occurrence.

Siblings were in this group together and alliances seemed to be forming. I saw both the boys and the girls being hostile and aggressive toward each other. It was obvious that the students would get frustrated quickly, and several had taken to communicating by gestures of aggression. Someone would spit in someone's face and a classroom

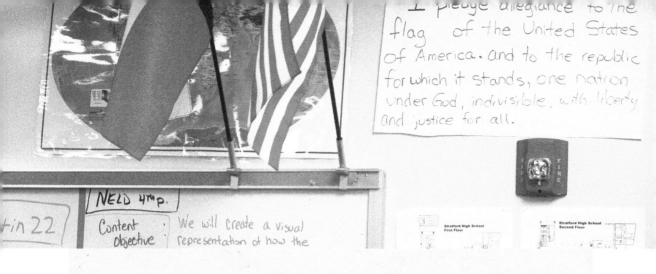

brawl would break out. This type of thing was also happening in some of the other classrooms and on the school bus. Several students in the general population told me that they were scared of this new group. We knew the campus needed more support but there was no funding to provide an extra teacher.

There was talk across the district of these rowdy newcomers and what a hopeless problem it was for the campus. To its credit, the school had set up a schedule where these students could have intensive ESL instruction for the first four hours of their day. The campus had a math teacher with an elementary background, so they were fortunate to have a fundamental math class. But all of this resulted in a segregation from the general population for most of the day. It seemed necessary for the safety of all the students.

And, again, more under-schooled newcomers continued to enroll!

Toward the end of October, my director offered me the chance to work part time at this campus. I would be there every day to support the campus in any way that made sense.

I said yes immediately, which seemed crazy to many people that I knew.

But I had been trying to figure out why the situation was so hard to manage, and this was an opportunity to roll up my sleeves and help find a solution from "the trenches." I was excited to work with the staff. We all had experience with differentiation for ability levels, with poverty, with second language acquisition, with behavior issues, and with social and emotional needs. The problem here seemed to be that this group of new students came with all of that and a lack of norms of formal education.

I received a great deal of support from the principal and other administrators as well as our Bilingual/ESL department. For the most part, I was asked to focus on the refugee group. Our team was given a great deal of flexibility.

We did some rearrangement of the classes and I initially took about 20 of the older students. Katherine Dierschke joined the team as a long-term substitute for one of the ESL teachers. She was getting her teaching certification, and her background with immigrant youth was a blessing to these children.

Once my new class was settled into a regular schedule, I implemented "circle time" to allow anyone who wanted to share an opportunity for authentic language production. By then many of the students understood basic English, and it turned out to be a great place to start learning about classroom norms. This was one of our first conversations. The students wanted to talk about the bullies who were trying to fight with them in the apartments. Those bullies happened to be a group of Hispanic students.

A student named Francies had joined our class from Ethiopia. While he did not have literacy, he was able to speak quite a bit of English and would often talk on behalf of the students.

Francies said to me, "You are a good Mexican, Ms. Salva. But some Mexicans is not good. They try to fight with us every day. I don't fight them. I move little ones away from them."

"You know that has nothing to do with being Mexican," I told him. "Young people are sometimes afraid of what they don't understand. I'm very proud that you don't fight with them. I'm sure it's very hard to walk away."

Then his intention became clear to me. "My mom told me, 'If you get to your good and wonderful life in the United States, don't get into any trouble.'"

"She didn't come with you? Is she still in Ethiopia?" I asked him.

Francies paused and looked down, "She died, Miss. She died a few months ago before we come here."

"Okay," I thought. "I am NOT prepared for this. I am not qualified. There are over 30 refugee middle schoolers who have all been through some type of war and displacement. They had already lived through such hardship. Of course they are acting hostile. They have no common language. They have been through so much. There are so many issues here. How will I help them?" I was so worried that I would fail them.

But what I did have was a strong desire to help them be successful. They could see that. They realized from day one that I believed in them. And I wasn't alone. Everyone around me wanted what was best for the students. This gave me hope, and I was confident that if we kept an open mind, we could all grow and learn together. *Carol*

THERE ARE A FEW CHALLENGES CRITICAL for teachers to understand about the SIFE population. I do not want to waste your time and go into depth because most teachers realize those immediately. For example, how do I teach a biology lesson from the textbook when the student is unable to read in their native language, much less the English in the textbook? The higher the grade level, the more overwhelming it may seem to work with a student who has low levels of literacy, or who has had interrupted formal education.

For me, it was actually a blessing to have so many students with this background all together at one time. As I got to know the students, I realized that each one of them brought so many different talents and gifts to our classroom. In efforts to find alternative ways to assess students' comprehension levels – it dawned on me that some of the activities (creating representations, comparing and contrasting, making connections) were exactly what we were trying to get our mainstream students to do. The students who were SIFE demonstrated they were indeed capable of working at grade-level. In fact, they each had gifts that should be a welcome addition to any classroom.

Students who are SIFE have often lived a life laden with challenges, and have overcome hardships such as having to leave their home country because of war, or simply not having enough money from day to day. When you survive that type of hardship, you prove that you can do difficult things.

We can't underestimate the power in this. Many of their grade-level, mainstream peers have never experienced such hardships. Teachers and parents are wracking their brains to figure out how to build "grit" in today's youth, as it is such a direct predictor of success later in life (Duckworth, 2016). The irony is that under-schooled students embody qualities that contribute to this "grit." They already know how to persevere and keep going even through challenges.

It's critically important to understand that the students with interrupted formal education bring so many qualities and important perspectives to the table. They have experience. They have value. They have voice. We can leverage their gifts in our learning communities. Without romanticizing their situations, we must keep in mind that their hardships, like any challenges, bring perspective. Their personal histories may impart them with certain strengths for learning as well.

If a student has been out of formal schooling for some time, we wonder where they were. They were somewhere. And that somewhere, may well have been a place where they struggled to meet their basic needs for survival. It stands to reason that these young people lacked access to the technology (e.g. electronic tablets) that their American peers take for granted. This does not mean, however, that they are at a great disadvantage cognitively.

If we study the work of Jane M. Healy

and Nicholas Carr, it becomes apparent that this lack of technology may provide certain advantages for developing cognitive function. In her book "Endangered Minds: Why Children Don't Think and What We Can Do About It" (1999) Healy examines how television, video games, and other components of our culture negatively impact a child's ability to concentrate, absorb, and analyze information. In Carr's book, "The Shallows" (2011), he describes ways in which the Internet alters our brains and neural pathways. He warns that use of technology creates a means of artificial memory, which may hinder our cognitive abilities.

Like many parents, I am saddened by the amount of screen time allotted to my children. And with the Internet, I know that something we have given up is the need to wonder about things. A Google search may answer nearly any question we ask, in effect replacing our curious and imaginative minds. The research of Healy and Carr reminds us that there are pros and cons to everything. If you have lived many years without these modern conveniences, you may have spent more time doing things that promote wonder, and strengthen cognitive skills.

While technology can provide our students with extensive background knowledge and virtual experiences, the relationship between technology and cognitive abilities is complex. Students missing significant amounts of schooling may lack the extent of background knowledge traditional students possess. This lack of opportunity does not equate to cognitive delay. Students labeled "SIFE" have little or limited formal education, but they have been learning. Like every child, their unique background and perspective can enrich our classrooms. **They experienced a lack of opportunity, but not an inability to learn.**

As educators, we have access to resources illustrating this phenomenon, but have we shared this knowledge with our students? Understanding the difference between 'lack of opportunity' and 'inability' is not enough for educators; we must also act on it. The best way to do so is to be explicit with students who are SIFE, explaining why we implement specific techniques to aid their learning, and how embracing their own "grit" can translate to success. Furthermore, metacognitive strategies extend content and background knowledge, as well as promote language acquisition. Our middle school and high school students who are SIFE are mature enough to understand metacognitive strategies. When we employ appropriate techniques, and students understand why those techniques work, their belief in their abilities begins to change as well.

In some instances, the older the SIFE student is, the more difficult it may appear to educate him or her at the appropriate grade level. Let's consider, however, that the older the student is, the more capacity he or she has for understanding metacognitive strategies. We will delve into these considerations as we progress through the book. ●

PART I

WORKING WITH STUDENTS WHO ARE SIFE

WHO ARE SIFE/UNSCHOOLED/ UNDER-SCHOOLED STUDENTS?

AN INCREASINGLY DIVERSE POPULATION is altering the makeup of our classrooms, and posing a challenge for teachers striving to meet the needs of every type of learner. A growing subset of ELLs (English Language Learners) who require specific attention are unschooled or under-schooled students, commonly referred to as SIFE (Students with Interrupted Formal Education) or SLIFE (Students with Limited or Interrupted Formal Education). In this book we will use the term SIFE to eliminate confusion.

Students in this category are generally newcomers to the United States who have interrupted, minimal, or no formal education from their native country. Circumstances such as war, natural disaster, poverty, political turmoil, and lack of transportation/ resources can contribute to students' limited educational experiences.

Some students who are SIFE are also categorized as migrant (students who have worked for several years to support their family financially, in an industry such as agriculture) or asylee/ refugee (students who emigrate to the United States for fear of persecution in their home countries). It is important to note, however, that not all refugee students are identified as SIFE.

Newcomer/ Recent Immigrant	Students who came within the current or previous year from another country.
Asylee or refugee	Students who have been forced to leave their country in order to escape war, persecution, or a natural disaster.
Migrant	Students who move from place to place following agricultural work.
Long-Term ELL	Students who have been an ELL 6+ years in U.S. schools.
SIFE	Students who are a Student with Interrupted Formal Education.

The majority of SIFE students are enrolled in grades 6-12 and are faced with increasingly challenging academic content and standardized testing requirements. In addition to needing solid instruction in literacy and numeracy skills, they also need broader orientation into our public school systems, procedures, and basic learning and study skills. **These students depend upon the classroom teacher, the school community, and the community outside of the school walls to facilitate their orientation and integration into their new learning environment.**

Since students who are SIFE students often lack basic reading and writing skills in their native languages, teachers need to be prepared to teach language, in addition to content, to maximize English language development. Sheltered Instruction (SI) strategies in content area classes, and quality ESL/ESOL instruction are necessary to ensure that students have extensive opportunities to interact with the English language and receive comprehensible input and scaffolded opportunities for output.

At the heart of quality instruction, it is crucial that teachers of students who are SIFE possess an understanding of culturally responsive teaching in order to provide appropriate empathy and an enhanced, safe, and interactive environment for optimal language learning and academic achievement.

	REFUGEES MAY	OTHER ELL IMMIGRANTS MAY
Immigration Experience	• Come to the U.S. due to fear of persecution in their home countries • Flee their home countries without saying good-bye to family members • Leave their home countries quickly due to apparent danger and have no time to gather important documents for traveling • Live in refugee camps in countries near their home countries while waiting to be processed for resettlement to the U.S. • Have learned skills in survival and decision-making due to multiple exposures to involuntary or dangerous situations and issues	• Come to the U.S. for a variety of reasons, such as joining family members or for a better livelihood • Leave their home countries by choice and have opportunities to say good-bye to family members • Leave their home countries by choice and have enough time to gather all important documents for traveling • Learn survival skills and decision-making through normal life experiences
Experience in U.S.	• Resettle in the U.S. often without the support of any family members (nuclear or extended) • Need opportunities to learn basic literacy skills to accelerate their learning	• Settle in the U.S. with the support of family members (nuclear or extended)
School / Language Experience	• Have varied camp experiences • Come from refugee camps that may not be well organized • Come from camps that may lack the basic necessities of life, food, or housing • Lack the ability to read or write in their own language or English	• Have had a range of educational opportunities • Have access to a range of basic to modern necessities of life in their home countries • Have a range of reading/writing skills in either their own language or in English

Resources: *WIDA Focus on SLIFE: Students with Limited or Interrupted Formal Education. (2015)*
ELLs in Texas: What Teachers Need to Know. (*2015*)

EVERY STUDENT HAS A STORY...	ELL	Asylee/ Refugee	SIFE	Migrant
OMAR — Syrian, educated in Arabic, high degree of L1 literacy, displaced due to war, spent several years in Jordan	✔	✔		
KAYSHA — Born in Congo, spent years in refugee camp in Uganda, not allowed to attend 'church' school, native language is Swahili, no L1 literacy	✔	✔	✔	
TOMAS — Born in Dallas, educated in U.S. until 2nd grade, family moved back to Honduras. Spent 4 years not attending school, some L1 literacy	✔		✔	
CECILIA — Born in U.S., 6 months of the year in Iowa, 6 months of the year in Texas, has missed more than 3 years of school, had to say goodbye to her parents, home language is Spanish	✔		✔	✔

WHAT DO I NEED TO KNOW ABOUT WORKING WITH SIFE?

HOW DO I WELCOME MY NEWLY-ARRIVED STUDENTS THAT ARE SIFE?

The value of providing a warm, welcoming environment for new SIFE arrivals to your classroom cannot be overemphasized. They may or may not share a home language with you or other classroom peers. You may or may not be able to communicate with them in their home language. Their ability to communicate in English will range from nonexistent to near full proficiency. Their understanding and experiences of school culture will vary.
By ensuring that your classroom is a place where students feel instantly welcomed and supported, you enhance their first experiences as a student and facilitate their learning.

It may sound simplistic, but training yourself to wear a pleasant expression as a "default" in the classroom goes a long way toward a good first impression. A genuine smile (that reaches the eyes) sends a clear message to the student: "You are important. I am glad you are here." This is also where your outlook on teaching students who are SIFE as an additive experience rather than as a deficit experience comes into play. We will explore this topic later in the book when discussing growth mindset and the benefit of having SIFE learners in our classrooms.

After the introductions are made between you and the SIFE student, your next task is to introduce them to the class. As a

ELLs in Texas: What Teachers Need to Know (Seidlitz, Base, Lara 2015) effectively outlines and explains systems and suggested procedures for welcoming newcomers into the classroom. The sections below have been modified to include the unique needs of SIFE and unschooled/under-schooled students.)

WHAT SHOULD MY CLASSROOM LOOK LIKE?

Remember, for some SIFE and unschooled students, your classroom may be the first time they experience a structured classroom setting. Consider how you would want to be welcomed, and what you would want to see, if you were in a similar situation.

The physical arrangement of classroom furniture and desks also contributes to the overall classroom environment. Seating students in cooperative groupings can break down barriers and encourage conversations between students. Teachers often agonize over the perfect arrangement of desks that can work for different learning tasks. It is worth noting that in many classrooms, students from grades 3-12 are changing desk arrangements in under one minute. Students in my class practiced this for one class period to help save instructional time and minimize disruption. The "Desk Olympics" video (**Bit.ly/deskolympics** or use the QR code on the next page) shows SIFE and newcomer students from my class as they learn to rearrange desks into cooperative groups. Grouping is important as many teachers realize that shoulder partners and smaller groups allow students to rehearse their English, and to ask for assistance of peers easily. The use of targeted peer assistance allows a selected student to provide limited, "just in time" help to a student that is struggling to understand instruction or tasks. Keep in mind that students who provide this support are students first; they are not teachers.

rule, unless you have advance information that they have the proficiency necessary, it is wise not to ask the student to say anything other than their name and their native country, if not born in the United States. You want to set a tone of low risk regarding verbal output, since many of these students are self-conscious about their pronunciation of English. They may also have reservations and feel stressed about talking and interacting in a public-school setting. You are setting a tone for future interactions, and a friendly, non-critical approach works best.

DESK OLYMPICS

Use the QR code to view a video showing SIFE and newcomer students from my class as they learn to rearrange desks into cooperative groups.

You might find it useful to stand at your classroom door and imagine yourself as a student who has not yet experienced the school setting. At first, the student may not be familiar with some things that are common in effective classrooms. But over time, many aspects of your environment can help them feel linguistically and emotionally supported. Examples are colorful posters on the wall, visuals, shared writing and other environmental print, information posted regarding daily assignments, student work and objectives for the current lesson.

Some teachers label common school items in multiple languages in the classroom. When norms and/or expectations are posted on the walls, they should be done with visual supports and scaffolding to ensure that all learners understand the expectations. It is considerate to give the student a classroom tour as soon as possible. This is a great opportunity to utilize someone in the community who speaks the student's native language. If not possible, there are free apps such as Google Translate that convert spoken English into a different spoken language.

Having a folder with your handouts for your classroom (i.e., norms, expectations, homework policy, and make-up policy) ready for new students is very helpful. If

you can provide this information in the student's home language it would be even more useful. A map of the school showing where your classroom is located helps them navigate the hallways. There may be new arrivals throughout the school year. This is an excellent opportunity for your "veteran" newcomers to take a leadership role in your classroom. Appointing a willing ambassador is beneficial for the newly arriving student as well as the veteran student who is now valued for his authentic contribution to the class.

It is vital that you build a classroom community that respects and values diversity among students. No student should be worried about ridicule or rude peers in your classroom. This may seem like an impossible task with some age groups but it is not as difficult as you would think. We are advocates of implementing a social contract for any classroom and revisiting it often. Our recommendation is to have the students create the norms together without any rules imparted by the teacher. This can be a powerful tool as students often set high expectations for themselves when given ownership of this process. For this to be effective, students must believe that accelerated learning is possible in your classroom, under the right conditions. For more on the social contract, see page 45.

WHAT IS CULTURALLY RESPONSIVE TEACHING, AND WHY IS IT NECESSARY WHEN TEACHING SIFE?

According to Geneva Gay (2010), "culturally responsive teaching means using the cultural characteristics, experiences, and perspectives of culturally diverse students as conduits for teaching them more effectively."

Teachers of SIFE who are culturally responsive provide an enhanced environment within which students may practice, play with, and perfect their English language development and understanding of school culture. Students in these classrooms feel safe in practicing language structures, asking for assistance, and interacting with others. With increased interactions, they can internalize easy to acquire features of English and acquire cultural cues and social skills that help them to better navigate the school environment.

Culturally responsive teachers can act as cultural brokers for students who are SIFE and their families as they navigate the "ins and outs" of U.S. schooling. For these new arrivals, it is very helpful to know that the teacher values their primary language and culture, and views them as resources for the class, rather than challenges or obstacles.

In the culturally responsive classroom, teachers ensure that their students use their native language to help one another, interact socially in group work, make connections between their first language (L1) and the target language (L2), respect one another's cultural norms, and check comprehension.

CULTURALLY RESPONSIVE TEACHERS ARE:

✓ Socio-culturally aware

✓ Positive towards students from diverse cultures

✓ Committed to more equitable schooling for culturally diverse students

✓ Capable of providing instruction supports in a challenging educational context

✓ Interested in learning about their culturally diverse students

✓ Committed to creating an inclusive, welcoming learning environment for all students

✓ Possess an additive perspective about the presence of ELLs in the classroom

HOW DO I EMBED PRINCIPLES OF CULTURALLY RESPONSIVE TEACHING INTO MY INSTRUCTION?

Your classroom is a place where all students, especially students who are SIFE, feel valued and respected. The process for building this environment may include some additional learning on your part and an intention to teach in a culturally responsive manner. As teachers, it is important to examine our attitudes towards these students for any subconscious bias or stereotyping.

Culturally responsive teaching is more than posters on a wall or food tasting opportunities. If you are comfortable doing so, you might begin by sharing your culture and heritage with your students. Many teachers offer family information and other personal facts about themselves to their students to begin the relationship building process. You should also consider the age of your students and the content you are teaching. There may be appropriate opportunities to honor culture and heritage learning in thematic units for your content area.

Because each student is unique in their history and life experiences, we should make a point to learn about their culture and traditions. We can begin with any intake information gathered by the school or welcome center. Although during initial enrollment, this information is important, it does not tell the whole story. It would be wrong to assume that everyone from a country, religion or native language share the exact same traditions or customs. Team building activities, student surveys or simple conversations with the student can help you learn more about students' culture.

Through building relationships with the communities that support your students, you send a strong message of respect to

COMMUNICATION TOPICS FOR TEACHERS AND PARENTS/CAREGIVERS

✓ behavior

✓ explanation of classroom norms and expectations

✓ requesting assistance with completion of work

✓ celebrating accomplishments

✓ suggesting resources for use at home

✓ requesting classroom assistance from parents

✓ inviting parents to share their knowledge or culture

the students and their families. Communicating with parents and/or caregivers in the language they prefer may require a translator or translation technology. This extra effort will go a long way in building relationships. Communications with parents and/or caregivers should cover a wide range of topics. As with any family, these parents should receive information about behavior and classroom norms and expectations. Communication can also include celebration of accomplishments and requests for support with completion of work. Teachers or school staff may send resources for use at home and may also request classroom assistance from parents. Our parents are wonderful resources to share their knowledge or components of their culture as it relates to instruction and concepts being taught. In this way, a culturally responsive classroom incorporates the "funds of knowledge" and "lived experiences" of students and their families.

Teachers should learn a few words in the languages of the students in their classes. This can be quite fun as students observe their teachers exhibiting similar behaviors to their own as they are learning English.

Teachers of students who are SIFE can be more culturally responsive by providing materials in the students' native languages and promoting the ongoing development of these home languages. Literature and other texts in the classroom can reflect multiple ethnic, linguistic and cultural perspectives to the extent it makes sense, given the subject/course. Displaying and incorporating pictures, books, labels, and other information from different cultures makes the learning environment more enjoyable for all students.

Developing an awareness and appreciation for the cultures of other students in the class breeds a respectful learning environment. As a teacher, you are responsible for setting that tone and building expectations of behavior that support it. Students who are SIFE, who feel safe in the classroom, will more quickly adapt to U.S. schooling, and be more capable of handling the challenges they face in acquiring and learning English, mastering the required curriculum, and understanding school culture.

LEARNING ENOUGH ENGLISH TO SELF-ADVOCATE

Osama had been in my class only a few weeks when he learned enough English to say: "Ms. Salva, my math class- very easy for me. I need change." He understood when I explained that the English of math is what would be most difficult for him and why he may not be as successful in an English math class.

Shame on me for my low expectations, but I was operating under the results of his initial mathematics testing from a few months earlier. Osama was very respectful, but continued to advocate for himself until I spoke with his math teacher who agreed with him, and so I finally called our district's Welcome Center and asked them to please retest him. Osama passed our placement tests for his Algebra Class and also for Geometry and was moved to the next level up, which is Algebra II. He is functioning well in that class with a bilingual dictionary, and an intense desire to do well. – *Carol*

Osama was an inspiration - many of my students are now asking for retest opportunities. From this experience, I learned how valuable it is to understand a district's intake process. Each district has a different intake process, whether it is located at a newcomer center or at the front desk of your school. If your district operates a newcomer center, the intake process may provide a great deal of information. If you are a teacher with new arrivals and your system is not set up to provide you with this information, you are not alone.

Regardless of how thorough the intake process, teachers must get to know their students and allow them time to demonstrate what they already know. Many of our students who are SIFE come from traumatic circumstances and may not be able to perform optimally at the time of intake assessments.

Knowing the results of these assessments and intake inquiries is an important first step in becoming acquainted with our students who are SIFE. From there we can create an environment where students can demonstrate to us what they are able to do.

If your school district does not have a newcomer center that shelters newcomers for their first courses and focuses on establishing basic academic and social English, consider scheduling secondary students in a way that allows for additional time in ESL/

ELD courses. Some states provide credit-bearing innovative courses for ESL students. Many secondary campuses offer additional reading or literacy electives, which can allow for scheduling blocks with the same teacher. Thoughtful scheduling may provide benefits similar to those of a newcomer center while students interact and learn with the general population.

HOW CAN I ASSESS THE ENGLISH PROFICIENCY AND BACKGROUND KNOWLEDGE OF STUDENTS THAT ARE SIFE?

Aside from being aware of the English proficiency levels in listening, speaking, reading, and writing for each student who is SIFE, you will need access to any diagnostic testing gathered on new ELLs used for identification and initial placement.

Results from any oral language proficiency test that the ELL might have been administered upon entering the district reveal ELLs' ability to speak and comprehend spoken English. These results provide helpful information with regards to levels of social and academic English. Getting to know the student in a classroom setting will allow you to better assess these students' abilities in comprehending content, following directions, and asking questions.

The required English language proficiency assessment results (published by most states) offer a glimpse into the ability of ELLs to comprehend text. As a benchmark, continue to reference and utilize test results to measure students' progress and advancement towards higher levels of proficiency over time. Just as with other ELLs, one of our primary goals with students who are SIFE is to ensure that they make progress towards full proficiency in English each year. By using language-based benchmarks and other diagnostic probes, teachers can monitor and track students' progress towards this goal.

Knowing levels of knowledge and skills of arriving students, as well as identifying strengths and deficits that may not be revealed through initial diagnostic testing and English language proficiency assessments, is valuable. ELLs who are unable to speak enough English to participate meaningfully in state-approved entry and placement tests can still share what they know through tools designed for their population. For example, the Refugee Intake Assessment in the Texas Student Refugee Framework: A Collaborative Approach (Obamehenti & Seidlitz, 2013) addresses a broad range of student academic background knowledge. Although designed specifically for refugees, this tool can be useful with other populations of students who, for various reasons, miss significant amounts of schooling.

REFUGEE-FOCUSED INTAKE PROCESS

This process ensures an initial task and observation component divided into three domains: Cognitive, Affective, and Language

(1) Affective: Limited English proficient students shall be provided instruction in their home languages to introduce basic concepts of the school environment and to instill confidence, self-assurance, and a positive identity with their cultural heritages. The program shall address the history and cultural heritages associated with both the students' homes and the United States.

(2) Linguistic: Limited English proficient students shall be provided instruction in the skills of comprehension, speaking, reading, and composition both in their home languages and in English. The instruction in both languages shall be structured to ensure that students master the required essential knowledge, skills, and higher order thinking abilities in all subjects.

(3) Cognitive: Limited English proficient students shall be provided with instruction in mathematics, science, health, and social studies both in their home language and in English. The content area instruction in both languages shall be structured to ensure that students master the required essential knowledge, skills, and higher order thinking abilities in all subjects.

The result of the initial intake assessment is then used to design a Refugee Achievement Plan (RAP) for each refugee student. Due to the various unique backgrounds of refugee students, each student will have an individual RAP that is customized to yield the best results for that refugee student. Furthermore, the RAP contains short and long term goals that allows for foreseeable achievements.

Following is a suggested informal initial language skills assessment that leads to the design of a RAP for a specific refugee student having minimal formal education. It is important to note that the result of this informal initial language skills assessment is only an indication of the possible level of proficiency for the student.

If the student has no language skills at all, is completely unable to communicate, uses gestures like pointing instead of speaking or reading, certain steps must be taken.

Use the results from the Observation and Goals columns to design the Refugee Achievement Plan (RAP). Specify some short terms goals and some long term goals. For example, a short term goal could be: The student will be able to know his or her way around the school without any assistance from peers or teachers.

This intake form was created in accordance to the §89.1210 Texas Bilingual education program content and design. The code states that the bilingual education program shall address the affective, linguistic, and cognitive needs of limited English proficient students.

SIFE ACHIEVEMENT PLAN

Name

Date

Parent/Guardian/Adult contact

Gender

Age

Language

Country of Origin

Translator

Observer

Results from state-
approved assessments

Other relevant information

COGNITIVE (I)			
TASK	**OBSERVATION**	**GOALS**	**RESOURCES**
Ask student to sort cards by color.			
Ask student to sort cards by living/non-living things.			
Ask student to sort cards by number and alphabet.			
Ask student to sort cards by plants/animals.			
Ask student to identify/ describe continents/oceans and other features of a world map in first language.			
Have student solve/explain (numerical) math problems based on grade level.			
Ask student to identify date on a calendar and time on an analogue clock.			

AFFECTIVE (2)			
TASK	OBSERVATION	GOALS	RESOURCES
Ask student about his/her school experience. Have you attended school? How many years of school have you attended? What do you do well? What difficulties do you have in school?			
Ask student: Who do you live with, and where do you live?			
Ask student: Which three people do you talk to often? What are they like?			
Ask student: What do you like to do when you are not in school?			
Ask student: (after school tour/lunch): What do you see in school? In the cafeteria?			

LINGUISTIC (3)			
TASK	OBSERVATION	GOALS	RESOURCES
Ask student to spell his/her name in first language.			
Ask student to read in first language.			
Ask student to write a description of what he/she likes/dislikes.			
Ask student to tell or summarize a favorite story in first language.			
Ask student to describe his/her current knowledge and experience of English.			

In Texas, the Austin Independent School District (AISD), empowers teachers with information critical to meeting the cognitive, affective, and linguistic needs of their students who are SIFE. They created an online system called the LPAS (Language Proficiency Assessment System) to efficiently gather the necessary demographic and educational history data of newcomers enrolling in the district (SIFE as well as non-SIFE). Lupita Narvaez of AISD's Multilingual Department spearheaded the effort in order to help teachers gain access to relevant information at a time when the district is facing an influx of newcomers to the district (especially at the beginning and intermediate language levels). With the new system, not only do classroom teachers have instant access to information about their students' years in U.S. schools, asylee/refugee status, and languages spoken at home, but also to instructional interventions that teachers can immediately implement to boost the achievement of their students who are SIFE.

Implementing an online system with easily accessible data as well as targeted instructional accommodations benefits both teachers and students. The data can be entered into the system in the first days that the new student is present in school by an LPAC (Language Proficiency Assessment Committee- a system used in Texas to manage decision-making for ELLs) representative.

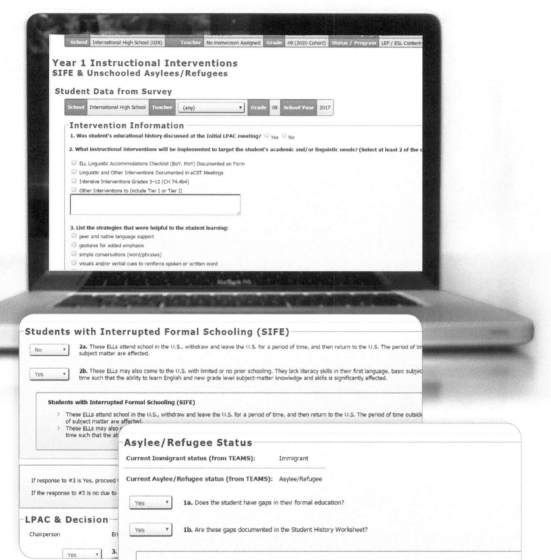

Year 1 Instructional Interventions
SIFE & Unschooled Asylees/Refugees

Student Data from Survey

| School | International High School | Teacher | (any) ▼ | Grade | 09 | School Year | 2017 |

Intervention Information

1. Was student's educational history discussed at the Initial LPAC meeting? ○ Yes ○ No

2. What instructional interventions will be implemented to target the student's academic and/or linguistic needs? (Select at least 2 of the c

☐ ELL Linguistic Accommodations Checklist (BoY, MoY) Documented on Form
☐ Linguistic and Other Interventions Documented in eCST Meetings
☐ Intensive Interventions Grades 3-12 (CH 74.4b4)
☐ Other Interventions to Include Tier I or Tier II

3. List the strategies that were helpful to the student learning:
☐ peer and native language support
☐ gestures for added emphasis
☐ simple conversations (word/phrases)
☐ visuals and/or verbal cues to reinforce spoken or written word

Students with Interrupted Formal Schooling (SIFE)

| No ▼ | **2a.** These ELLs attend school in the U.S., withdraw and leave the U.S. for a period of time, and then return to the U.S. The period of tir subject matter are affected. |

| Yes ▼ | **2b.** These ELLs may also come to the U.S. with limited or no prior schooling. They lack literacy skills in their first language, basic subjec time such that the ability to learn English and new grade level subject-matter knowledge and skills is significantly affected. |

Students with Interrupted Formal Schooling (SIFE)

> These ELLs attend school in the U.S., withdraw and leave the U.S. for a period of time, and then return to the U.S. The period of time outside of subject matter are affected.
> These ELLs may also
> time such that the ab

If response to #3 is Yes, proceed
If the response to #3 is no due to

LPAC & Decision

Chairperson   Eri

| Yes ▼ | 3. |

Asylee/Refugee Status

Current Immigrant status (from TEAMS):   Immigrant

Current Asylee/Refugee status (from TEAMS):   Asylee/Refugee

| Yes ▼ | 1a. Does the student have gaps in their formal education? |

| Yes ▼ | 1b. Are these gaps documented in the Student History Worksheet? |

Unschooled Asylees/Refugees

These ELLs are determined to be unschooled asylees or refugees in accordance with state-established criteria. These students lack lite trauma as a result of their previous circumstances. It is highly critical that this category be coded accurately for proper identification of

To qualify as an unschooled asylee or refugee, each of the following criteria must be met:

> The student must be identified as limited English proficient (LEP) as defined by state law in TEC, Section 29.052, and must partic
> The student's permanent record file must contain appropriate documentation of asylee/refugee status. The student must
>> be an asylee as defined by 45 Code of Federal Regulations, Section 400.41 or a refugee as defined by 8 United States Co
>> have a Form I-94 Arrival/Departure record, or a successor document, issued by the United States Citizenship and Immig
webpage includes a TEA form that may be used in the rare case that a campus has compelling evidence of a student's a

Online Language Proficiency Assessment
System created by Austin ISD

PART II

UNDERSTANDING
GRIT & GROWTH MINDSET

GRIT

At the beginning of 2016, I happened to be on Twitter when I came across Mike Butcher. Mike is the editor-in-chief of TechCrunch, so he's quite a famous personality in the UK, or globally, if you are in the tech world. He was tweeting about a new effort, "Techfugees." I was immediately inspired by this. He was organizing volunteers who wanted to contribute their technology talents to help the refugee crisis in some way. It was a live streaming event with different people talking about different ideas.

I came into class the next day, and we turned on the live stream – now everyone was inspired! Soon after, we decided to participate in the "Hour of Code." Every child in the world should have an opportunity to learn to code. I knew this would be a challenge as some of my students were not yet able to read independently. I looked into it and found that there were opportunities for non-literate students. Even a four year-old could code with these free apps! The Hour of Code is a global movement to have all children introduced to computer science.

There was one problem; my students didn't want to use the 'babyish' app with no language. One student, Hamsa, was adamant about doing the Star Wars program and going through the 15 levels of coding that every other student was being challenged to do.

I hesitated – he didn't even have foundational math skills. He didn't know right from left in English. Coding requires right, left, up, and down commands. There were so many things we had yet to teach him and I was worried that we were setting him up for failure.

But who am I to hold him back from trying? I decided that if he really wanted this, I would help him as much as possible. Anyone who wanted to code would get

as much help as they needed to participate. We made a great **video**; to watch it, use the QR code at the right or visit this link: **bit.ly/Tech4SIFE**

We sent it to Mike Butcher who loved it! Techfugees is now a strong global movement and they use us as an example of how tech can propel the learning of under-schooled refugees. We are the example of what is possible!

A child's desire and motivation and MINDSET supersede almost everything. If you want to do something you'll go the extra mile and you'll put in more effort. You'll find yourself in what Csíkszentmihályi calls "flow"(2008). And learning will come spilling in all around you.

I think I learned as much or more than they did that day.

– Carol

WATCH CAROL'S NEWCOMERS ENJOYING THE CHALLENGE OF CODING

GRIT IS A VERY HOT TOPIC IN EDUCATION right now. In her book *Grit, The Power of Passion and Perseverance*, Angela Duckworth (2016) explains that it is grit, not a person's IQ that predicts success in life. Grit is what propels people to continue working toward success. Her TED talk has been viewed over 8 million times and her research has been leveraged by educators around the world. In that talk, Duckworth admits that while grit is extremely important to cultivate, we are not yet quite sure how to accomplish that.

I find this ironic as many of our under-schooled students already embody grit and perseverance. Students with limited schooling often come with life experiences that required overcoming challenges with persistence. But do they understand the power of this strength? Isn't it worth pointing out to the students that many parents and educators are desperately trying to build this trait in today's youth? Isn't it worth showing our students the power of their grit? Isn't it worth explaining that they have qualities that could be a huge advantage over the typical middle or high school student?

According to Merriam-Webster, the concept of grit can be defined as a firmness of mind or spirit; unyielding courage in the face of hardship or danger. Our students can relate to that definition. We suggest sharing that definition in the context of a class discussion. Teachers can then demonstrate to students the power of grit in the context of achieving academic success. As professionals, we typically define grit as a person's passion for a particular long-term goal, coupled with a powerful motivation and persistence to achieve that goal.

Passion. Persistence. Motivation. Those are key predictors for success. As our students come with the proven ability to persevere, my main job becomes motivating them and identifying what they are passionate about. We have seen many students learn quickly and become passionate about reading and learning once they understand and embrace the concept of grit.

Lack of formal education may seem to be a bigger issue in the upper grades; however, these students do have advantages.

Once we explain how the mind works, and how grit is a key predictor to success, we expand students' interest and potential comprehension. An older student can more easily grasp potential outcomes, understand metacognitive strategies, and see how learning can be accelerated by specific actions and effort on their part.

With older students, educational gaps often appear wider and thus time in secondary classrooms may even feel futile. Nothing could be further from the truth. The reality is, the older the student, the more we can capitalize on their maturity as a learner. We can't look at their developing literacy in the same manner that we would for an early childhood learner, as an elementary age emergent reader does not have the same capacity for understanding metacognitive strategies.

Consider also that older students come with more of a sense of urgency, and often have a deeper appreciation for educational opportunities than their younger counterparts. These emotions become the internal drivers to their awareness and acceptance of the value of grit applied to their studies.

GROWTH MINDSET

Educational gaps are not limited to ELLs labeled SIFE. By the time I was in high school, a series of poor choices had left me many grade-levels below my peers in math and reading. When I gave effort in school I often struggled to understand the concepts. With each wrong answer I felt as if I was not as smart as the other students.

I remember teachers telling me that I had more potential. I thought it was nice of them to think that, but they just didn't realize that I was not as smart as other kids. I believed in my heart that I was "bad at math" and that I was a "poor reader." This attitude affected my effort and played out negatively in how I performed academically.

I finally did graduate, albeit a few years late. I remember the day things turned around for me.

It was my first day in Houston Community College. I was sure this was a huge waste of time, but my mother was forcing me to go.

That day, a bizarre thing happened. The professor asked me to help some older students who were struggling because they had not been in school for many years. I was astounded. I wasn't usually asked to help anyone academically. I obliged and started reteaching what we were learning to these other students. Not only did this help me deepen my understanding of the content, but I was also being treated with respect by the instructor and the class.

I used to think that junior college was easier than high school. Now that I know more about how we learn, I can see that it was not.

The reality was that my mindset changed. I started believing that I could get smarter about these subjects. With that belief came more effort and with more effort came more positive reinforcement.

I was the first person in my family to earn a bachelor's degree. I went on to get my Masters' in Educational Administration. I am looking forward to starting my doctoral work in the field of education and I can't help but appreciate what I'm learning about how our minds work and what is possible for every child... if they believe. – *Carol*

The power of mindset is a concept that can be shared with all children. Our under-schooled students face many obstacles but none that are too great to overcome. The key is that we believe it is possible to overcome these challenges and communicate this belief to our students consistently. Just as important is for our students who are SIFE to believe that academic success is possible for themselves.

There is an old saying that "If you believe you can do it, you're right. And if you believe that you can't do it, you're right." The research of Carole Dweck goes deeper into this idea. Carol S. Dweck is a Professor of Psychology at Stanford University. After decades of research, Dweck introduced her theory on growth mindset and is now renowned for her work on the mindset psychological trait.

Dweck's work impacts education because, at a foundational level, she has shown us that teaching a growth mindset creates motivation and productivity. There is tremendous power in believing that we get smarter and better with continued effort. If we teach students that their thinking is key to their success, we are helping students to persevere and learn from their mistakes. This is a mindset that will serve them in education and other areas of life. We believe, and our students believe, that success in math is not about being "good at math" but rather the belief that a person can "get better at math" with effort.

We are well served if we challenge our own mindset beliefs regularly while also intentionally challenging the mindset beliefs of our students.

Students labeled as SIFE are generally upper elementary and older. These students are mature enough to comprehend this idea. Like us, they can comprehend this concept and why it works. But as educators, we must be explicit when teaching growth mindset and other metacognitive strategies.

Dweck (2015) wrote an article for *Education Week* in which she identified positive outcomes she was observing from her research on growth mindset. In addition, she shared the misunderstandings and pitfalls that were also arising as a result of teachers implementing her ideas. Among them she cautioned this:

" A growth mindset isn't just about effort. Perhaps the most common misconception is simply equating the growth mindset with effort. Certainly, effort is key for students' achievement, but it's not the only thing. Students need to try new strategies and seek input from others when they're stuck. They need this repertoire of approaches—not just sheer effort—to learn and improve."

This "repertoire of approaches" that Dweck mentions is critical for our students who are SIFE to succeed in an academic setting. However, trying new strategies and working cooperatively with others is not something that we would encourage for only our students with limited formal education. This effort should be a part of a classroom culture that benefits every student, but is understood to be crucial for students who are SIFE.

5 WAYS TO DEVELOP GROWTH MINDSET WITH SIFE

1) **Don't underestimate any student's strong desire to learn.** Sometimes we limit our students to tasks we believe are within their zone of proximal development (see Hamsa's story on page 32). With scaffolding and support, a student can exceed even their own expectations, as well as ours.

2) **Educate students on the power of grit and growth mindset.** If our students who are SIFE already have some traits of grit, do they know it? Do they know the research about the ability to overcome obstacles and persevere? Do they understand grit and how it is a predictor for success in life? Do they know how fast they can learn if they want to put forth the effort? These are conversations that are worth having often.

3) **Understand that mindset and grit alone is not enough.** We have to be ready with resources like appropriate reading materials, native language resource support, instructional technology, and extra learning opportunities that SIFE learners will need to close their educational and informational gaps.

4) **Use Examples of Success That Promote Growth Mindset.** A quick Google search reveals many examples of refugees or immigrants that have not only overcome challenges, but made a difference in our world. These articles are the perfect non-fiction text to use with students for shared reading.

   Look for people in your community. **In this video** (**bit.ly/GersonVideo1**) of Gerson Bermudez, a SIFE student who learned a significant amount of English in seven months even though he came to America without his parents, was living in a low socioeconomic area, and was in classes with mostly Spanish speakers. Gerson has helped many teachers and students understand the importance of growth mindset.

5) **Teach metacognitive strategies.** Be explicit and spend time reflecting on the process of learning. The focus should not only be on the facts being learned, but on how to learn the facts. *Understanding HOW we learn* is empowering, fosters independent learning, and fuels a growth mindset. As part of this teaching, regularly ask students to explain their thinking pathways. They need to learn and practice this language as much as they need to learn the academic language of their content-area courses.

BENEFITS OF HOSTING AN INTERNATIONAL STUDENT

By the fall of 2016 I was teaching a newcomer class with students who were SIFE at Stratford High School in Houston's Spring Branch ISD. A few months into the school year the faculty was offered an opportunity to have German exchange students come present to any classroom that wanted to learn more about the German lifestyle.

We jumped on this! I chose "German Traditions" and "Refugees in Germany" from the choices the students had offered.

The German guests presented their topics with visuals, but despite this we stopped multiple times to clarify meaning and ensure that the information was comprehensible to my class.

My students were fascinated. They were very gracious as the exchange students talked about both benefits experienced as well as problems faced by so many refugees coming into Germany. They told personal stories that included both perspectives.

We thanked them for their time and had a class discussion after they left. Many of our refugee students asked if they could please create a similar presentation to tell about a refugee's journey from their own perspectives.

No longer did I have to figure out a way to make technology relevant to their learning. The students went around me to figure out how to use Google slides and other means of presenting with technology. Our librarian obliged when we asked if students could come in after school to get more familiar with computer skills.

We had to have class discussions before our presentations to make sure that everyone wanted to see what was being presented. Students could opt-out if they were uncomfortable with images of war or immigration hardships.

There's a fine line between honoring someone's experience and re-creating traumatic events for students. In our case, everyone was very interested to see and hear about the journeys of their classmates and what each had to overcome. Because I tweeted about it, we were invited to contribute to a project by a fifth grade classroom in Laos. They are compiling migration stories and my students were honored to contribute their stories to increase awareness and understanding for those students. – *Carol*

> "Language learners and international students are valuable members to our project. They bring perspectives we do not have. They add value and contribute in ways that are important for a global view."
> – *Dr. Jon Lohse, archaeologist for CEI and co-founder of the San Felipe de Austin Heritage Learning Project, speaking about Spring Branch ISD newcomers.*

When talking about growth mindset, another point to consider is not only the expectations we have of our SIFE and underschooled students, but how we regard them as new, diverse, and interesting additions to our classroom makeup and school community, much like we would international exchange students.

Research on best practices of culturally responsive teaching is a fairly new area in the field of education. It is understandable that many educators may have concerns and apprehension about teaching and supporting students who are SIFE in their classrooms. When teachers integrate culturally responsive approaches with such students, they find there is nothing to fear. Instead, they have the opportunity to help integrate these students into our culture and come to view the students as a benefit and treasure for enlightening native English speakers. Newcomers, including the SIFE newcomer, can bring the class exposure to other languages, cultures and perspectives, that deepens learning for everyone.

For more evidence of this, consider the idea of foreign exchange students. Have you ever hosted an international exchange student? Why would someone do that? What are the benefits to us, to our children, if we host international exchange students? The following common responses are listed on the World Education Program website: **bit.ly/WEPbenefits**

- Acceptance and understanding of an array of different cultural and community perspectives.

- Awareness and adoption of alternative, multi-faceted approaches to learning.

- Analytical and problem solving skills.

- Enhanced interest in global issues as well as a broader general knowledge.

- Prospective employers in almost every field look favorably upon knowledge obtained of another language and culture.

- Increased pressure to communicate and relate to others develops an awareness of group dynamics and personal sensitivity towards others.

Parents and educators want to grow global learners that are well prepared for the 21st century workplace. Is it any wonder that people go to great lengths to give their children experiences with foreign exchange students? How is this different from our international newcomers, many of whom are SIFE, being in our classrooms?

I have seen many of these benefits play out among my SIFE students and more that I am adding to my own list. For example, my students are an excellent example of appreciation for education. When I heard a mainstream middle school student say he was "inspired by how much the refugees are learning and doing," I realized that something special was going on.

GLOBAL LEARNING *and* BREAKING GEOGRAPHIC BARRIERS

> "My class loved playing the Kahoot about your holiday traditions! They immediately started wanting to find the different countries on the map! It was such an enriching experience!"
>
> —*Natalie Krayenvenger, 4th grade teacher in Baltimore, Maryland*

My students give back. Over the past year, we have done service projects, and their experiences and international backgrounds provide a unique opportunity to help educate other students far and wide. When given an opportunity to connect with other classes, my students are regarded as "experts." Their first-person accounts are mesmerizing. Learning becomes reciprocal and global thinking is enhanced on both ends.

This type of learning is innovative and can seem as if it would require a great deal of preparation. In fact, facilitating this can be much easier than you might think.

As the winter holidays approached, my students had many questions about my family's traditions. I decided to create a lesson that would honor everyone's celebrations. To begin, I showed them images of "Day of the Dead," a holiday celebrated by my family who are from Mexico. I then gave each student a Kahoot paper template to identify one fact about how they celebrate a special holiday in their country or culture. Many of my students come from countries with conflict. Several told me that it was nice to show something positive about their country and customs.

It was fascinating to learn about Children's Day in Japan. Who knew that many families in the Congo eat cake and dance in the evening on Christmas? Our Muslim students stumped us with dates and customs about Ramadan and Eid al-Adha.

I wish you could have seen their pride when they saw their questions come up in the game.

Now that would have been great enough. But thanks to the world of Twitter and Facebook, we were able to share this Kahoot with teachers all over the world. And not only did we share it… classrooms that played it connected with us to tell us what an enriching experience it was for them. See this tweet from the awesome Ms. Francis whose class played even though they are over 1,000 miles away. She sent a video clip!

Emily Francis
@emilyfranESL ☐ Follow

@MsSalvac watch my Ss' engagement playing your Ss game! 😭 thank you for sharing! @wmirvinelem
play.kahoot.it/#/k/a7ce776e-b…
10:26 AM · 21 Dec 2016 · North Carolina, USA
↩ ♺1 ♥2

But that's not all! Another amazing outcome from this one Kahoot was that Ms. Krayenvenger's class in Maryland not only played (she said her kids LOVED it and pulled out the world map right away) they also sent us some questions. Now, let's remember that I work mostly with newcomers and students that are SIFE. So you might think that it would be a challenge for us to respond. Not at all. They were so awestruck that these children almost 1500 miles away wanted to know things about them! My students were pulling out the bilingual dictionaries and translators to find the English words to write back to Ms. Krayenvenger's class. Before I realized what was happening, this one Kahoot turned into an authentic collaborative learning activity for both classes.

Kahoot is a free platform and I encourage teachers to utilize the tool for more than reviewing content. When students create a Kahoot, we have challenged them to use many higher order thinking skills. And this one Kahoot became the springboard for so many more. – *Carol*

It is exciting to see these students as they accelerate their learning and close their academic gaps. I appreciate global and authentic learning opportunities, because we are not just here to close gaps in academic skills. **These students demonstrate to others what is possible with hard work. We balance that with the kinds of experiences that will inspire to become future leaders themselves. Any of our students have this potential, and the kids in my classroom have expressed a strong desire to be a positive change in the world.**

How do you grow future leaders? As educators, we encourage the continuous development of intellectual curiosity, creativity and global thinking. My students who are SIFE have helped me so much in cultivating this mindset. I am constantly looking for "out-of-the-box" opportunities to engage my students in learning. The students themselves inspired me to teach this way. With older students who are SIFE, there is a synergy that can develop between teacher and students that becomes very powerful for everyone.

IDEAS FOR ENCOURAGING CURIOSITY, CREATIVITY, *and* GLOBAL THINKING

IDEA: Easily Gamify Your Classroom with Kahoot
Games can be a great way to get to know your students, support content area learning, and honor different cultures. Kahoot is a free game-based learning platform that is highly engaging for students. In 2016, there were only six countries in the world where someone did not play a Kahoot. **(www.getkahoot.com)**

Many educators have tapped into the power of gamifying reviews of content with Kahoot. But there are deeper uses of the platform, especially for learners that are ELLs and SIFE.

One example is to create a Selfie Kahoot.
Step 1) Teacher creates a selfie Kahoot that students play to get to know their teacher.

Step 2) Each student comes up with a Kahoot question about themselves to contribute to a class Selfie Kahoot (kahoot planning pages here: **bit.ly/KahootTemplate**).

Step 3) Play it, then share it with the world on social media. (With student names changed if necessary.)

Extension: Just before the holiday break your students can create a "Holiday Traditions" Kahoot that can also be shared with other classrooms around the world.

Content Classroom Extension: Have students create Kahoot questions (with correct answers and distractors) based on grade-level content they will be learning). This act of creation is a high level of cognitive function in learning.

Carol Salva is a Kahoot Ambassador, and her innovative ideas for using Kahoot to teach language and content are being shared by the company around the world. For more ideas, visit: **bit.ly/KahootESL**

IDEA: Mystery Skype with a Mystery Class
Join other teachers here: **bit.ly/MysterySKYPE**

Your classrooms will connect and play "20 Questions" to determine the others' geographic location. This is a fantastic opportunity for newcomers to get to know their new country. I knew it was going very well when I heard a student who is SIFE say, "But they just said that they were east of the Mississippi River!"

IDEA Mystery Skype with a Professional
Invite a professional to play the 20 questions with your class. He/She is only allowed to answer yes or no. Your class must continue to ask questions until they guess the profession of their online guest.

IDEA: Partner with Historical Professionals

Local historians, authors, archeologists, and state and government agencies have agreed to connect with our students. Some of our students have intimate knowledge about push/pull factors, migration, Civil War, etc. that provides them an advantage in traditional history classes. At the same time, they are filling in gaps of background information specific to the United States. We seek opportunities to have visitors and trips to historical landmarks to help our students build background knowledge for history standards that will be assessed. Participating in this form of learning enables SIFE students to have an opportunity to practice the English they want and need to fully embrace the experience. Many students are eager to talk about the parallels and connections that they make.

IDEA: Partner with Business Professionals

We had the founders of PledgeCents offer to help us raise funds for our classroom. This was incredibly helpful. Additionally, we used this as an opportunity to have them visit and share a presentation about entrepreneurship. The students were excited to ask their questions about entrepreneurial opportunities in America.

IDEA: Flip a Visit to a Local Business

Along the lines of entrepreneurship we were introduced to owners of a local restaurant. They were gracious enough to host us and answer our questions about owning a business. Chef Mike even did a demonstration on the logistics and economics of using every part of a pork shoulder that was recently purchased. Knowing that science classes were covering heat transfer, we made sure to use academic language in our preparation for this trip. Our students prepared presentations about cooking their native dishes and some of the students presented this at the restaurant. As an ESL teacher, I was focused on transition words and writing of procedural text. Read about the students' restaurant visit in the Heights Leader Newspaper: **bit.ly/HEIGHTSarticle**

IDEA: Virtual Field Trips

Some trips are published on the web while others can be created by you and your class. I recently visited Galveston, Texas, which is about an hour south of our school. I made a simple 3 minute video for my students as a hook to a lesson on ecosystems. Students are highly engaged when they see their teacher on location somewhere. You can then encourage students to record and share short videos of their weekend activities. The videos can be compiled and published to YouTube to show the perspectives of recent immigrants in their new country.

IDEA: Invite School or Community Newspapers to Feature Students who are SIFE

A journalist for our school newspaper did a very inspiring piece on the international students and the benefits they bring to our community. Requesting the questions ahead of time helped the students prepare for the experience. We reviewed the questions as a class to be sure the students understood the questions. The students used paragraph frames to write responses and it became a meaningful writing assignment for them. The online version of the paper is planning a continuing series so that our students can continue to educate and inspire our community.

MORE IDEAS SPECIFIC TO NEWCOMERS WHO ARE SIFE CAN BE FOUND ON MY BLOG
bit.ly/SalvaBlog

SOCIAL CONTRACT

At the beginning of 2016, a team of researchers visited my class to observe instruction and learning of SIFE students. Several of the African refugees that I had taught the year before were in high school now, and were no longer considered "newcomers". Those still in our area had made significant progress and were put in sheltered classes for intermediate students. We tracked a few of them down so that these researchers could interview them about the significant turnaround in their educational experience the year before. Every student mentioned two factors that played a significant role in their learning.

The first factor was reading as much as possible. To facilitate the students' reading, we located resources that were:

- Leveled with simplified text.
- On topics of interest that are compelling to the students.
- Related to cultural information (theirs and others).
- Written in English, or sometimes in their native language.
- Tied to topics for research and inquiry.
- Intended to close gaps in background knowledge.

The second key factor was the social contract that we put in place from the very beginning.

I was not surprised by this at all. Our social contract was truly the beginning of learning opportunities for our class. When I first met them, this group had been hostile and fighting daily with one another. The administrators reported that a refugee student was being sent to the office every single day. One of our first effective strategies with these learners was the implementation of a social contract. I saw the dramatic change in their behavior immediately and these students count it among the most important factors in their success.

I first learned about the idea of a social contract from visiting Joseph Maurer's math classroom several years ago. Maurer is an award winning master educator who was showing impressive results with low socioeconomic, second language learners. As an ESL specialist, I noticed that his data stood out impressively with this demographic. When I visited with him we reviewed the previous year's standardized test scores of his students. Many of them were below grade level, not unusual for second language learners. Several of these students had not passed their math classes the year before, yet somehow, through Maurer's instruction that year, he was closing gaps and showing impressive standardized assessment data for these same students. When I observed his classroom it was evident that he implemented a great deal of sheltered instruction strategies and offered a significant amount of opportunities for discussion and writing about math. He incorporated "7 Steps to a Language-Rich Interactive Classroom" (Seidlitz & Perryman, 2011). He also included several innovative opportunities for students to think deeply about math. One significant thing I learned from him was the idea of a social contract.

The social contract is a key element not only for behavior management but also to propel learning for all students. When students take ownership of their learning environment, they feel safe, they feel honored, and the class begins to function in a productive way.

– *Carol*

CLASSROOM NORMS *and the* SOCIAL CONTRACT

Consider the students' buy-in when they are the ones creating the rules for the classroom.

In creating a social contract, the teacher facilitates a discussion about how the students should treat one another, how they should treat the teacher, and how they would like to be treated. The key is that the students identify each norm and each norm is understood and agreed upon by all.

One of the challenges often faced by learners who are SIFE is their apprehension to take risks which can be interpreted as an unwillingness to participate. Many factors can contribute to this, and it is critically important to develop a classroom culture that helps them feel safe and supported in producing the target language. Assisting the students to create a social contract is the first step toward building a learning environment where students feel comfortable participating immediately in class.

In addition to feeling safe, learners who are SIFE need to have clear guidelines for classroom behavior. They need rules, but they must also feel respected, and like any student, they should be treated with dignity even if they are new to these rules or new to formal education.

When I was asked to work with the group of refugee students at the middle school, they were already at a point where they were being hostile to one another. Some were quite aggressive. Many were shoving, hitting and spitting in each other's faces. Classroom brawls were breaking out daily.

These students were understandably frustrated. They needed clear norms for how to function together as a class. We were attempting to impose classroom rules but a critical piece for these learners (and every learner) is that they take ownership of their learning and the norms of their learning environment.

One of the first effective strategies for this group was the implementation of a social contract. This type of contract is effective in different grade levels, demographics and subjects. It has been effective in kindergarten classrooms, so it stands to reason that any group of students can describe appropriate classroom norms for a productive learning environment.

Soon after the social contract was in place, everyone settled down and began functioning together in a productive way. When asked later, these same students attributed a great deal of their success to their social contract. It was not a set of rules imposed on them. It was a set of norms created by them.

STEPS TO IMPLEMENTING A SOCIAL CONTRACT

- Assume all kids want to learn. Once you offer them an opportunity to participate in a class where they are successful, they will surprise you with the expectations they set for behavior.

- Use the following 4 questions (simplified for SIFE students) from Capturing Kids' Hearts (Flippen Group, www.flippengroup.com).

    1. How do you want to be treated by your peers?
    2. How do you think your peers want to be treated by you?
    3. How do you want to be treated by the teacher?
    4. How do you think your teacher wants to be treated by you?

- Offer these questions one at a time. Make sure the students understand the question and provide a sentence stem and possibly a word bank for them to use in the ensuing collaboration with other students. Ensure that students spend adequate time thinking about their response to the stem and copying it. The students first talk with a partner, then with someone across the room, and finally with a third person. They should write down the responses they receive.

- Facilitate a class discussion about the norms they are developing for the classroom. Make sure students understand the term, "norms." No contributions are included in the norms unless all students agree on them. None of the norms are set by the teacher, but the teacher is responsible for pointing out if any norms are against school policy or are not possible to enforce.

PART III

ACCELERATING LANGUAGE DEVELOPMENT

Before I went back into the classroom to help with the refugees, I had been working with students on a learning project with archaeologist, Dr. Jonathan Lohse. Initially, I didn't think that I would be able to continue this project, given my new population of learners. The students I had been working with before were highly engaged and offered insightful feedback to Jon's team and the Texas Historical Commission (THC). I didn't know if my students who were SIFE would be able to participate as fully in the experience.

As it turns out, their perspectives were also highly valued by Jon and his team. Our project with the THC opened my eyes to the idea of Heritage Learning for my students that are SIFE. This concept provided an unexpected way to engage them in learning about history and the heritage of their new surroundings and to leverage their unique perspectives as immigrants and refugees to deepen everyone's learning. Archeology provided excellent opportunities for thematic units because of the real-world uses of science, math, and history. This lends itself well to culturally responsive teaching.

By being culturally responsive, I mean that I wanted to honor their culture. According to Geneva Gay (2010), culturally responsive educators implement lessons that allow students to see themselves in what is being taught. By doing so, they create a safe and accepting environment that fosters appreciation for their culture and that of others. I wanted my students to know that it is important to learn more about their heritage and that it is also important to learn the history, heritage and culture of people in their new environment. (For more information about culturally responsive teaching, see page 19.)

Jon introduced me to a colleague who was from Nigeria. At that time, Dr. Tunde Babalola was completing his doctoral studies at Rice University and agreed to visit our classroom. This was one of the first times that I was able to document the second language acquisition techniques I had been using.

Use the QR code at the right to see a **video (bit.ly/ArcheoVisit)** showing how we prepared for Dr. Babalola's visit. Knowing that my students were pre-literate, but had a strong desire to communicate with the visitor, inspired me to provide sentence frames that were authentic for the students to practice. The video shows how sentence frames provided scaffolds for authentic speaking, reading and writing which supported oral language development and emerging literacy. – *Carol*

SEE HOW SENTENCE FRAMES SUPPORT
ORAL LANGUAGE DEVELOPMENT AND
EMERGING LITERACY.

SECOND LANGUAGE ACQUISITION BASICS

When teaching students who are SIFE, it is important to keep fundamental second language acquisition basics in mind. These practices must be the foundation of lessons we plan if we want to provide effective opportunities for English language development.

Understanding how language is acquired sets the foundation for truly differentiating instruction to meet the needs of ELLs. This is especially critical for students facing linguistic challenges and gaps in formal education. Knowledge of comprehensible input and the role of the affective filter is essential for best serving students who are SIFE as well as other language learners.

In *ELLs in Texas: What Teachers Need to Know* (2015), Seidlitz et al. provide a comprehensive overview of the key second language acquisition principles that are essential to understand and implement when working with second language learners. The following sections below have been modified to include the unique needs of SIFE and unschooled/under-schooled students.

WHAT IS THE DIFFERENCE BETWEEN LEARNING A LANGUAGE AND ACQUIRING A LANGUAGE?

Understanding the difference between learning and acquiring language is very important when it comes to the English language development of SIFE who are ELLs. Students are not learning English as an "elective," but rather acquiring the language as a means of communication in their new culture. Language learning involves studying and memorizing the vocabulary and grammar of a target language. Students produce written and oral language and receive feedback from an instructor.

Language acquisition involves receiving copious amounts of comprehensible input with low stress opportunities for output in a target language. The only way for students to achieve high levels of fluency in English or in any target language is in receiving sufficient amounts of oral and written input, coupled with opportunities to express themselves orally and/or in writing in authentic contexts. It is not possible to achieve proficiency by studying vocabulary and grammar alone. This is especially significant for students who are SIFE because it affects how we focus our instructional time. Time should be focused on providing many opportunities for oral and written interaction rather than intensely focusing on vocabulary lists and finer points of grammar.

WHAT IS COMPREHENSIBLE INPUT?

Comprehensible input is any written or spoken message that is understandable to a language learner because of the context. The phrase "comprehensible input" is part of Stephen Krashen's theory of second language acquisition. According to this theory, humans learn a new language primarily by receiving new messages in language that they understand because of the context.

Krashen (1985) wrote that input was best received when it was slightly challenging for the language learner. If the input was not challenging at all, no language development would occur. If it was too challenging, the language learner wouldn't understand the message. Being immersed in a language you don't understand is not an example of comprehensible input, but incomprehensible input. Instead, learners should be exposed to language that is slightly challenging and engaging.

WHY IS PROVIDING COMPREHENSIBLE INPUT ONE OF THE MOST IMPORTANT FACTORS IN SECOND LANGUAGE ACQUISITION?

Without comprehensible input, language development does not occur. Students must receive sufficient comprehensible input before they will be able to spontaneously produce real output in a target language. It is crucial that all teachers of ELLs understand how to effectively increase comprehensible input so that their students will more quickly advance in language proficiency.

WHAT IS "COMPELLING INPUT" AND WHY IS THE CONCEPT IMPORTANT?

Compelling input is a term Stephen Krashen (2011) uses to describe input so interesting that the language learner forgets that it is in a different language. The learner is relaxed, engaged, and focused on meaning. In order to provide compelling input, teachers must make sure they provide listening and reading experiences that are highly engaging and interesting to the students, and that contain some input that is at and slightly above the student's current level of language proficiency.

GENERATING COMPELLING DESIRE FOR OUTPUT

Each student is unique and possesses gifts to be shared with the world. I'm constantly on the lookout for unique and novel ways to engage them so those gifts can be revealed. The more compelling the input, the more engaged the students are with their learning. I take it one step further and look for experiences to provide them with authentic interactions that honor their intelligence and their unique perspectives. I refer to this as generating compelling desire for output. According to Stephen Krashen (2011), the easiest way to get students to receive comprehensible input is to offer them topics to read about that are not only interesting, but are also compelling.

In my experience, the same has been true when it comes to output. The more we honor our students' intelligence, the more of that intelligence they will show us. Who knew that one of my students had lived near an active volcano and knew four languages? Who knew that another student had been spending hours at home learning to code with C++ programming language? The more I discovered about them, the more possibilities I found for my students.

U.S. History Experience with Author, Dr. Paul Spellman

I recently met an author, Dr. Paul Spellman. Bryan McAuley of the Texas Historical Commission connected us. I told Dr. Spellman that my students enjoy learning about Texas history, but really need a deeper understanding of U.S. history. He wrote many famous books on Texas history, and has also recently published a wonderful book of love letters exchanged between a young couple during World War I.

Dr. Spellman has agreed to come and do some storytelling in my classroom. The students are so excited about his visit. He marked a few pages in his book that are appropriate for high school students. My class is working hard to read these passages with fluency so that we can make a video as a gift to Dr. Spellman when he comes.

Many of us became teachers because we wanted to inspire children to love learning. I feel so fortunate that my students who are SIFE allow me to see evidence of this daily.

An ESL teacher often has the luxury of using any content to teach language. Why not use the dramatic real stories of our history to teach language? And if you are the history teacher — why not use language to deepen their understanding of history?

I've done this a few times with archaeologists, scientists, and historians who were more than happy to connect with my class in some way. They can visit, they can correspond with your students, they can Skype with you, etc. They usually tell me that they are honored to do so.

—CAROL

The story opposite is an example of this. When I met Dr. Paul Spellman, I knew I wanted him to visit my classroom if possible. But the extra step is having the students record themselves reading passages of his book, as a gift for Dr. Spellman. That is the extra step that offers a compelling desire for output with these kids.

Another example is Natalie Krayenvenger's fourth grade class in Baltimore, Maryland. Not only did they benefit from playing our holiday traditions Kahoot (see page 41), but they were moved to send follow up questions to my students. My class spent time with bilingual dictionaries, electronic translators and the English they had been learning over the past few months to answer these authentic questions sent by this class. Several of them commented that they really liked the task.

One of my favorite examples of generating compelling desire for output was during our second week of the school year. Our friend Stephanie at the London headquarters of Kahoot asked if they could Skype with my class. I was incredibly nervous because everyone was a newcomer and we had only met twice in class at this point. I was afraid my class would not be able to communicate with the Kahoot employees. But the kids had already played a Kahoot with me and they were excited to talk to these people who were wanting to communicate from Europe. Google Translate came to the rescue. We spent a class period getting their questions documented. They took them home and practiced so that they would be ready the following week. I was inspired by their perseverance and efforts. Even our most shy student from Japan was proud to ask her questions, and happy to let me record her doing it.

Dr. Babaloa's visit to my classroom (page 48) was my first realization of the power of compelling desire for output. Dr. Babaloa was from Africa and was coming to tell the class about his studies in African archeology. Prior to his visit, the student in the video, Emmanuel, works so diligently to be understood. I did not have to prod or coax him to practice his English. Emmanuel was compelled to do it so that he could communicate with Dr. Babaloa. If you watch the video, you will see Emmanuel recount what he learned from the visit. He was not only proud to get his question answered, he learned so many things and eagerly shares his new learning in the target language.

I find it easier and easier to think with possibilities in mind. Once you see the huge pay off, you'll be looking for possibilities everywhere! – *Carol*

WHAT IS THE ROLE OF THE AFFECTIVE FILTER AND WHY AND HOW IS IT RELATED TO COMPREHENSIBLE INPUT?

The affective filter is a key component of Krashen's model of second language acquisition. It has been described as "an imaginary barrier" between a language learner and new input. The barrier consists of negative motivational and emotional factors that interfere with a learner's ability to receive comprehensible input. If a learner feels embarrassed and stressed about speaking in front of peers, it is difficult to receive comprehensible input.

Such an affective state is very prevalent among students who are SIFE and other beginning ELLs. To receive input, the language learner needs to be relaxed and concentrating on meaning and not on form. The more they are in a state of "flow" and are concentrating on the message, the more input they can receive. The more stressed they are, the less input they can receive.

This is why it is important for teachers of ELLs to ensure that they take steps to lower the affective filter of their students. For students who are SIFE, lowering the affective filter and creating a welcoming and safe environment for language output to be practiced is a non-negotiable.

HOW DO I LOWER THE AFFECTIVE FILTER FOR MY STUDENTS THAT ARE SIFE?

To lower the affective filter, teachers must create a low anxiety classroom for students who are SIFE. To do this, they need to help ELLs feel comfortable making mistakes and taking risks in using English.

SOME THINGS TEACHERS CAN DO TO LOWER THE AFFECTIVE FILTER INCLUDE:

✔ Avoiding public correction of errors

✔ Not forcing students to speak before they are ready

✔ Allowing ELLs to seek clarification in their native language

✔ Providing feedback on language production ONLY at the student's level of language proficiency (i.e., providing beginning ELLs writing feedback that targets the kind of language produced by Level 1 students, not Level 5 students)

✔ Providing frequent opportunities for peer interaction

✔ Creating a welcoming, culturally responsive classroom environment

✔ Getting to know the students' parents/guardians and maintaining an open relationship with them

WHAT ARE BEST PRACTICES FOR PROVIDING COMPREHENSIBLE INPUT FOR STUDENTS WHO ARE SIFE?

There are two sources of comprehensible input: aural (heard) and written. We will discuss each of these in turn. Aural comprehensible input can be provided by you, other students in the class, and by media. In order for students to receive effective aural comprehensible input from you, it is important to provide enough context while giving instructions and explaining academic concepts. Simple practices that help teachers provide comprehensible input during instruction include: simplifying speech, clearly explaining academic tasks, using speech appropriate for students' proficiency levels, and avoiding the use of idioms and regionalisms (Echevarria, Vogt, & Short, 2008).

To receive aural comprehensible input from other students, students who are SIFE need to interact frequently with English speakers and others at higher levels of language proficiency in a variety of authentic contexts. Structured, scaffolded activities where stems are provided can help students participate in conversations where they can receive "negotiated input" (i.e., clarification of English words and phrases that they do not understand).

To receive input from media, it is helpful to find high-interest sources. For example, television programs, music, and videos can be helpful. When watching video, many language learners find that they receive more aural input when the closed captioning is turned on so that they do not miss specific words and phrases used in authentic context.

WHAT CAN THEY READ?

High-Interest/
Low Reading Level books

Shared Texts created in class

Materials practiced in class

Books in the native language

Captions on TV shows/movies

Websites with Immersive Readers

News in Levels
http://www.newsinlevels.com

High-Interest/ Low Reading Level Books

Look for books that are highly engaging, but are written for students at lower reading levels. Some elementary non-fiction text may be high-interest but it is better to look for books that are more appropriate for adolescent youth. Leveled readers are often part of a language arts/reading adoption for your district. Collaborating with colleagues can help you present a variety of books to your students for free voluntary reading. In addition, Saddleback Publishing, **http://www.sdlback.com/hi-lo-reading**, and High Noon Publishers **http://www.highnoonbooks.com** are examples of publishers that offer leveled text that actually look like the types of books regular middle and high school students are reading. The topics are high-interest for this age group.

Shared Texts created in class

Set aside time to talk to students about common experiences. Examples are: What is it like to be in a new school? How can I learn quickly? What did you do this weekend? Will you be going to the pep rally… do you know what it is? From these conversations, you can brainstorm a bulleted list of ideas on the board. On chart paper, you can model a quick write from students' ideas. Take this one sentence at a time. Read the sentence aloud in a slightly slower than normal rate of speech, making sure to face the students to model some of the pronunciation. Next have the class chorally read the sentence. They copy these quick writes as a resource they can practice reading at home. Keep the quick writes posted in class. The walls should be dripping with language and text they can read.

Materials practiced in class

From our first day together, we are creating text together and practice reading it repeatedly. The first priority is to establish norms and provide ways for them to get assistance. We start with our Social Contract. We also create a simple "What to Say Instead of I Don't Know" poster so that students are able to start recognizing print in text that is meaningful and relevant to them. We review these frequently, reading them aloud, and discussing them in the context of the current learning context.

Books in the native language

Content specific books in the native language can provide an important native-language resource for students who are taking content classes in their second language. In addition, free voluntary reading in a primary language supports second language literacy. Additionally, every child with primary language literacy should have access to a bilingual dictionary or translation device if possible.

Captions on TV shows/movies

Teach students how to strategically watch English television: stopping the show to re-read the captions, rewinding to listen and practice pronunciation, occasionally looking up unknown words in a translation device.

Scripts from Yabla

This website has high-interest videos with features that allow you to track the captions, slow the rate of speech, pause and replay specific phrases. It can be successfully used in a center, and encourage students to use it at home. (It is a fee based program.)

News in Levels
http://www.newsinlevels.com

This site is fantastic for current news articles that are already adapted for ELLs. Each news article is written in three different proficiency levels. Readers are encouraged to master Level 1 (present tense and written with the 1,000 most common words) before reading the same story in Level 2 and then Level 3. The site offers a video with the text read aloud so every student is able to access the text. To introduce the site, I print out a story at Level 1 and we chorally read the article together. Next, I pass out Level 1 & 2 side by side and we read Level 2 and identify what is different about the two versions. (Verbs are in past tense in 2 and we discuss the changes.) Then I pass out the third copy that has all three levels so students can master Level 3 and also contrast it with the first two levels. It is important to model this progression to facilitate comprehension. Students will learn to take advantage of the scaffolding process when they work on their own.

CONTENT VS. ESL TEACHER

"But none of the other 8th grade Science teachers have refugees in their classes." This was the understandable response from Katheryn Stokes, 8th grade Science Teacher. Ms. Stokes had full classes and was concentrating on helping her students meet the increasing demands of the 8th grade Science state assessment.

From a classroom management perspective, at that time the group of refugee students posed a bit of a challenge, as they were known for their outbursts and disruptive behavior. From a scheduling perspective, the school planned to place the students into mainstream content-area classrooms for two-week increments.

Despite her initial apprehension, I am grateful that Ms. Stokes not only agreed to take them for two weeks, she also made them feel welcome and looked for ways to include them in meaningful activities.

After the two-week trial was up, Ms. Stokes asked to keep the students who were SIFE in her class for the rest of the year. She was impressed with their engagement and with the effectiveness of sheltered strategies she had used. The students were comprehending and functioning well in the class. Ms. Stokes recorded this quick **video (bit.ly/SIFEinSCI)** one day as she was showing me what kinds of anchor charts the students were creating and why it was important for the learning of the whole class. *– Carol*

WHAT IS THE DIFFERENCE BETWEEN TEACHING LANGUAGE AND CONTENT?

An effective content teacher uses language to teach concepts. An effective ESL or ELA teacher uses engaging content to teach the target language. This is an important distinction. Language is present in every classroom. But language and content goals play out differently if you are the Language Arts teacher vs. the Content Area teacher.

For the ELA or ESL teacher, there are many benefits to using grade-level content when designing thematic units. For example, a Language Arts teacher may decide to teach an archeology unit because of the rich opportunities for heritage learning and cross-curricular connections. There are multiple fiction and non-fiction reading choices and opportunities for authentic writing in such an engaging unit. Science and math concepts come into play as students deepen their understanding of timelines and environmental science. This is when the ELA or ESL teacher is using content to teach language.

The content teacher, on the other hand, is primarily responsible for teaching content. If they are a math teacher, the student must master concepts and practice math principles of math in class. A best practice for all content area teachers is to use academic language to strategically teach their content. Marzano, et al. (2001) tells us that there is a 19 point percentile gain in achievement if we allow students to participate in structured conversations about the content.

In the content-area classrooms, content is made more comprehensible for ELLs through teachers' knowledge and use of ESL strategies. As Menken and Kleyn (2010) state, "Regardless of the subject matter, all teachers must see themselves as language and literacy teachers and be prepared to teach language through content." The teacher is using strategies grounded in sheltered instruction. If the math teacher facilitates structured conversations and implements other sheltered techniques, it is an example of the content teacher using language to teach content.

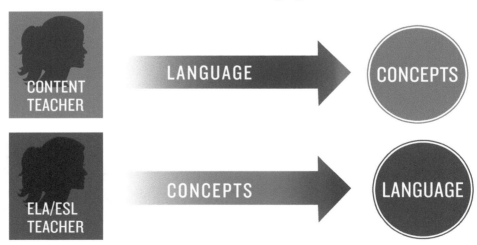

CONTENT TEACHER → LANGUAGE → CONCEPTS

ELA/ESL TEACHER → CONCEPTS → LANGUAGE

WHAT DOES THIS LOOK LIKE IN A CLASSROOM?

The teacher is using enhanced visual and vocabulary strategies, adapted texts, and structuring conversations and opportunities for reading and writing. In addition, the teacher is incorporating consistent checks for understanding and other methods of formative assessment. Content and materials are differentiated to meet students at their varying levels of language proficiency. The content itself is not watered down, but delivery methods are strategically in place to make content more comprehensible and to develop academic language for SIFE students. Essentially, teachers must teach their content as if it's a foreign language, while ESL teachers are helping students better learn and utilize the English language.

Conversely, in an ESL classroom, English language development should be the primary focus of instruction. While students are receiving academic content in other classes, the designated ESL/ELD time is when ELLs, newcomers, and students who are SIFE have the space to practice communicative competence, sentence structures, grammar, and acquire new English vocabulary. The ESL/ELD class is where students have limitless opportunities to engage in listening, speaking, reading, and writing, both in groups/pairs and individually.

See the charts below for comparison: When ESL and content-area teachers are collaborating, it is important to understand the different roles of teachers in different settings. The following chart clarifies the roles of ESL and content-area teachers in different settings.

ESL Teacher in an ESL Class	ESL Teacher in a Co-teach class	Content-area Teacher in Sheltered Class
Primary focus: English language structures and vocabulary	Primary focus: Linguistic accommodations of the subject matter for ELLs	Primary focus: Making content comprehensible for ELLs
Facilitate student interaction to develop oral language proficiency with specific English structures	Facilitate student interaction to develop oral language proficiency in the content area	Facilitate student interaction to develop oral language proficiency in the content area
Directly teaches high frequency social and academic English vocabulary	Teach academic and social English vocabulary related to lesson content	Teach academic English vocabulary related to lesson content
Provide daily opportunities for reading: teacher-selected and self-selected texts	Provide frequent opportunities for reading adapted texts related to content-area topics	Provide opportunities for reading adapted texts related to content-area topics
Provide daily instruction on specific language structures and opportunities to write using those structures	Provide linguistically accommodated opportunities to write about content-related topics	Provide linguistically accommodated opportunities to write about content-related topics

In the Sheltered Science Classroom

The 8th grade science classes were studying earth layers, tectonic plates, magma, and
a host of other concepts that seemed overwhelming for me to teach our new students.
But we were tasked with teaching grade-level
science concepts and I was determined to find
a meaningful way to do this. As I struggled to
find images and tie the unit together, it oc-
curred to me to show them the volcanoes in
Africa as a hook to my lesson.

This is when Lydia pointed to the place on the map where her family lived for a
short while. It was Tanzania and she struggled to describe what it is like to live
near active volcanoes. I quickly helped her find images to make her descriptions
understood by her classmates.

Everyone in the class was riveted as we listened to her story and took a quick virtual trip to the area using Google Earth. The content became dramatic and real
for us all in that moment.

I used this opportunity to not only teach content, but to create a compelling
desire for output. As it turned out, so many of our science concepts were not so
difficult to teach them. In fact, many students in the class had spent so much
time outdoors in foreign parts of the world, that they were able to help me easily
deepen the learning of the rest of the students. We made it routine practice to
illustrate our understanding of the concepts and take virtual trips to see areas of
the world where students were able to offer connections. As their sheltered science teacher, this provided me a chance to allow for a rich, interactive experience
for the whole class.

TOP 5 THINGS FOR **CONTENT** TEACHERS

✔ Get high quality, sheltered instruction training that emphasizes practical techniques like
7 Steps to a Language-Rich Interactive Classroom.

✔ Have kids verbalize to internalize content throughout the lesson.

✔ Chorally read something everyday (i.e. goals, sentence frames, vocabulary, etc.).

✔ Have visuals that you refer to throughout the lesson — your walls should be a co-teacher.

✔ Have students write at least one complete academic sentence in English everyday.

ESL Teacher Supporting Content Teachers

Some of our students who are SIFE were enrolled in a grade-level science class. When possible, I allow students to use our ESL time to create environmental print for our room or for the room of their content teachers. This is an example of a unit overview/input chart that was created by some of our refugee students during one lunch period in my room.

At the very least, students who are SIFE can list, label, and copy. That is exactly what was done here. Their science teacher,

Ms. Stokes, referenced earlier in this chapter, informed me that they would be starting the Earth Layers unit. We found this GLAD pictoral input **video** by Cliff Schaeffer (**bit.ly/ EarthLayersGLAD**) based on his work with Project GLAD. We watched the video and then stopped the frame at the end and covered the board with butcher paper. This allowed the students to trace the image and copy the academic terms.

My intention was to provide them an entry point into the content. It provided background knowledge for these students prior to their content lessons in mainstream classes. This activity prompted many questions that would later be answered in class during the unit of study and also facilitated much conversation, with grade-level academic language, about what they were drawing. The anchor chart was gifted to their science classroom where Ms. Stokes is an advocate of environmental print.

As an ESL teacher, my primary focus is on developing my students' English proficiency. It is a win-win when we can develop language and support content learning as well. – *Carol*

TOP 5 THINGS FOR **ESL** TEACHERS

✔ Challenge your beliefs. Plan or meet with like-minded professionals, even if it is your virtual professional learning network (ie: Twitter).

✔ Make sure everyone practices speaking in English EVERY DAY.

✔ Have everyone read every day in a way appropriate for their proficiency level.

✔ Find meaningful topics to help develop literacy.

✔ Have students set classroom norms that honor every student and respect his/her culture – (this will allow us to preserve every instructional minute).

ASSESSMENT

HOW DO WE ASSESS STUDENTS THAT ARE SIFE?

Assessing students who are not on grade-level can be perplexing. Teachers are often at a loss regarding assessment practices for students who lack the literacy to write or read at grade level. Before we can appropriately assess their learning, we need to be sure that we have taught our content in a comprehensible way. We must look beyond the activities we do and find ways to teach the requisite skills and knowledge in comprehensible ways. Ensuring comprehensible input is key for all learners, but it is essential for ELLs and for students who are SIFE. To read more about this, see page 51.

Let's look at assessment of non-English or limited English speakers before we discuss SIFE ELLs. As mentioned above, we must first ensure comprehensible input. Then we are ready to look for alternate forms of assessment that are in alignment with the language proficiency level of the student. For example, your non-English student may not be able to write an open-ended response about tectonic plates but there are several other ways he/she could demonstrate mastery of understanding. Examples include illustrations, labeling, creating a model, and use of native language to respond.

Most school districts have clear expectations and guidelines for assessing students with limited English proficiency. These guidelines generally require that we consider students' language proficiency using proficiency level descriptors that are identified and published for use by teachers. The proficiency levels are key to appropriately assessing language learners. If you understand what language skills students who are SIFE demonstrate most consistently, you can create an appropriate rubric or assessment that evaluates their knowledge of what was taught.

If our non-English speakers can be taught and assessed at grade-level, there is really no difference for our students who are SIFE, who are also language learners. We are able to provide instruction that is comprehensible to them. And we are serving them well if we can offer assessments and activities that allow their participation at their literacy and language level.

WHAT ABOUT SPECIFIC SUBJECTS?

The standards of some subjects, such as high school Algebra, are such that gaps in knowledge due to interrupted or insufficient schooling may prevent mastery of grade-level concepts by students who are SIFE in the same timeframe as on-level learners. District leaders, campus administrators, and teachers can create intervention plans to help students work to close gaps. Personal intervention plans for students who are SIFE should be communicated to the student and families. These courses may need to be repeated or even postponed by scheduling the student into a prerequisite course, but students can be successful with interventions that personalize learning based upon their specific gaps and needs.

SOME IDEAS INCLUDE:

Free websites that offer leveled math learning such as Khan Academy (free math video lessons offered in several languages)

Tutorials

Peer tutoring in English or native language

Center/work station approach to math instruction

Volunteer support

Structured Study Hall with Remediation Support

Summer school

Local libraries and outreach centers that may offer tutoring or support.

WHAT ABOUT ASSESSING STANDARDS THAT REQUIRE PREREQUISITE SKILLS?

The assessment of students who are SIFE will vary depending on the subject area and standards being assessed. Subjects such as chemistry or algebra require foundational knowledge for students to be successful. Mastery of standards in these courses can be demonstrated with alternative forms of assessments. For example, students can be allowed to show mastery in fewer equations or non-verbally (without text). But in courses such as these, a student who lacks the foundational skills may not be able to master the content without significant intervention.

Teachers must make every effort to shelter for language and make their lessons comprehensible. Students should be offered the opportunity to show mastery in different ways according to their proficiency with English. But if the teacher is sheltering for language and the student is still unable to master the standards, they should be assessed appropriately and grading should reflect the true mastery level of the content. If this occurs, a meeting should be conducted with the appropriate staff and teachers to decide if a change in schedule or course is indicated.

As stated above, this issue should be expected and schools should have an intervention plan in place for students who are below level with prerequisite skills. **If there is a plan in place, and the plan is communicated to the student and the family, the student who is SIFE is much more likely to persevere and take advantage of interventions.** They should know that some classes may need to be repeated but that their school has a plan for them that can result in academic success.

PART IV

IMPLEMENTING A PRACTICAL APPROACH TO INSTRUCTION

With such high standards being taught at every grade level, we wonder; what can a below-level language learner do in a grade-level class? What can students who are SIFE do in the middle school social studies class? Or the high school biology class?

When teachers are asked these questions, and they brainstorm a bit, the ones listed below are the top answers they offer. Ask yourself if you have seen a below-level learner engage in any of these processes:

    illustrating

      making a model

        acting out responses

          comparing things

            sorting things into groups

These tasks engage students who are SIFE at some of the highest cognitive levels we ask of our mainstream, grade-level learners. In the sections below we will discuss ways to develop academic language for students who are SIFE while engaging them at a high level of cognition.

We Are Just Like Gerson

People can learn English very quickly. We saw a video of a boy in Spring Woods High School named Gerson. He learned SO much English in 7 months. He did it with Duolingo and reading and practicing every day. So we are very much like Gerson. He is practicing for his future. He believes the task of learning English is important. So do we

LISTENING AND SPEAKING

I had shown my students the video of Gerson Bermudez more than once. This video of an actual immigrant student, reflecting on how he accelerated his English language acquisition, has never failed to have an effect. Students and teachers alike are inspired by the evidence of how a growth mindset can help us improve our learning at a rapid pace. Because of this, our class often discusses how we are similar to Gerson and what steps we should take to improve our own English.

This study of a real student overcoming the challenges of being a recent immigrant was highly engaging for my students. To meet speaking goals, I asked my students to think of questions they had for Gerson. I knew they would be compelled to produce language with an opportunity to communicate with him. Some of their questions needed to be translated but they practiced what they wanted to ask in English. This went well and it was fascinating to see how many of the students had questions about pronunciation and sounding like a native English speaker. Many wanted to know if he still had an accent and if not, how did he lose it? They wanted to know what he did and how long it took.

I love Gerson's reply to them. He explained that he still had his accent and he was happy to have it. He explained that it defined who he is, and often opens doors to discussions about culture. Use the QR code to see an an excerpt of that **video**, or visit **bit.ly/Gerson2.**

For me, this underscored the urgent need to have students producing as much English as possible in my class. I wanted them to have more opportunities to practice the language in a safe environment. It was obvious to me that many of my SIFE students who were newcomers did not like how they sounded and this would likely affect how much English they produced with me, and throughout their day. Many of my students were still in their "silent period." They were not comfortable yet producing independent English words and phrases. I simply had to create multiple opportunities for them to receive comprehensible input and then jump into the conversation when they were ready. We want to give the gift of academic language to every student. Giving my students who are SIFE compelling reasons and opportunities to use their new language is now at the forefront of all my lesson planning. — *Carol*

Though receiving comprehensible input is critical in the language acquisition process, encouraging language output is also highly significant.

When I provide professional development for teachers, I consistently echo the mantra: When students verbalize, students internalize. We encourage our students to speak in complete sentences, so they can practice proper academic language that can also transfer to academic writing. We teach our students that they can truly understand something when they can explain it.

We also want to emphasize why it is so important to create as many opportunities for students who are SIFE to produce English. From their perspective, they care about how they sound. From our perspective, we want all students to build oral language. The story of Gerson works to help teachers realize the value in having students who are SIFE engaging in various activities that encourage oral language production.

QSSSA
WHAT IS QSSSA?

One approach to scaffolding student/student conversation is Q, Triple S, A. The acronym stands for **Question, Signal, Stem, Share, Assess** (Seidlitz & Perryman, 2011). This activity gets students using all domains of listening, speaking, reading, and writing in a fun and interactive manner. QSSSA is beneficial for students who are SIFE because it occurs in a low-stress environment, where students have the wait time to negotiate meaning and practice responses with a partner before shar-

ing chorally with the class. Students are guided in their structured conversations by sentence stems and precise, easy-to-follow directions from the teacher.

WHAT DOES QSSSA LOOK LIKE?

This structure begins with the teacher asking a **question.** This is a great way to help students build academic language into their writing. The teacher can ask one question, or a short series of questions for the students to respond to. When they have a response ready, students are then asked to provide a total response **signal** to indicate to the teacher and the class that they are ready to move on. This could be a hand in the air, pencil on paper, standing up, etc.

The teacher then provides a sentence **stem** for the students to use with a partner for **sharing responses.** The stem could be as simple as "I agree/disagree because_____."

The activity ends with the teacher **assessing** the students by randomly calling on a few to respond, or rotating around to each group and asking for a response. See the chart on the next page for an example of the different variations that QSSSA can be used in different content areas, with varied response signals, stems, and methods of formative assessment.

STRUCTURED CONVERSATION

	QUESTION	SIGNAL	STEM	SHARE	ASSESS
MATH	What are some important things to remember when factoring equations?	Raise your hand when you can finish this sentence.	The most important thing to remember when factoring equations is... because...	Turn to your partner...	Randomize when calling on students.
SOCIAL STUDIES	Do you support Sam Houston's position on secession? Why?	Take your hand off your chin when you can finish this sentence.	I support/oppose Sam Houston's position because...	Share with the group.	Numbered heads together.
SCIENCE	What are some unusual characteristics of annelids?	Stand when ready.	The most unusual characteristics of annelids are... because...	Turn to your partner...	Randomize when calling on students.
LANGUAGE ARTS	Is Stanley a hero?	Put your pen down when you finish writing a response.	Evidence that shows Stanley is/is not a hero includes...	Inside Outside Circle	Journal Reflection

Sheltered Instruction Plus. Seidlitz, 2012.

ROVING PARAGRAPH FRAMES

WHAT IS ROVING PARAGRAPH FRAMES?

Roving Paragraph Frames is an activity that combines listening, speaking, reading, and writing in an engaging format to benefit all learners. For ELLs, it is essential to practice speaking and writing in English, especially in an environment that lowers the affective filter (see page 54) and enhances the ability to produce low-stress output. For SIFE and under-schooled students, the advantages of this kind of engaging learning environment eases learners into a classroom culture that is interactive and encouraging of language practice and growth.

This activity is successful because of its effortless use of grouping, randomization, structured conversations, and structured reading and writing opportunities. To give students who are SIFE as much exposure to various models/examples of spoken and written English, experimenting with various grouping structures is an excellent way to enable this practice in a low-stress environment.

WHAT DOES ROVING PARAGRAPH FRAMES LOOK LIKE?

This activity is excellent for all students and works very well for English learners. We first explain the activity and then provide an explanation of how it can be modified if you have non-English writers in your class.

TO FACILITATE ROVING PARAGRAPH FRAMES:

Give your students a sentence stem to begin the activity, and let them think and respond with a complete sentence. Sample: "It is important to understand the Bill of Rights because_____."

Ask the students to stand up with their paper and pencils when they have completed the written sentence.

Have the students "rove" around the room and find a partner.

Ask students to read their writing to one another. The first person reads his/her complete sentence, stem and all. The second person listens and then reads his/her complete sentence.

Ask students to write a new sentence that begins with a new stem, such as "In addition, _____." They can either "borrow or steal" their partner's response if it was different than their own or just create a fresh sentence.

Once sentence #2 is complete, partners raise their hands or stand back to back. The key here is to incorporate total response signals to indicate to the teacher that the task is complete. Now they are ready to rove again.

Have the students find new partners, and repeat the entire process with the second partner. ***It is crucial to instruct students to read everything they have written so far*** and for the partner to listen and then read everything that he/she has written so far as well. This validates student responses and encourages the use of listening and speaking skills. After reading individual sentences, students then write a third sentence with the stem "Also, _____."

To conclude, have students repeat the process one last time and rove to find their final partners. Once individual sentences are read aloud by each partner, ask students to write the final sentence using the last stem "Finally, _____." At this point, each student should have a well-constructed paragraph in hand, complete with transitions and complete thoughts recorded in academic English.

ROVING PARAGRAPH FRAMES FOR STUDENTS WHO CANNOT YET WRITE IN ENGLISH

Content teachers should be mindful of students who cannot yet write in English. For these students, you may decide to cluster them into a group so that you can work with them while the rest of the class is writing their initial sentence. You can use a native language peer, a bilingual dictionary, or translation app to get the students' ideas and help them complete the sentence frame. If the student is very new, it is beneficial to provide these students with the rest of the sentence frame so that they can participate with the rest of the class. You may also consider partnering your students for this activity so that your brand-new students are less apprehensive about roving and speaking. However you scaffold for your students who cannot yet write in English, know that the activity is still very meaningful for English language goals at the beginner writing level.

ROVING PARAGRAPH FRAMES FOR THE NEWCOMER CLASSROOM

If it is early in the school year, it is possible that your class with SIFE learners has a considerable number of students who are not able to complete sentence frames with coherence in the target language. Students should soon be able to complete simple sentence frames, but the reality for some of us is that we are receiving newcomers all the time and our classroom may be made up of many students who cannot yet write in English. Instead of having this activity become confusing for the class, consider taking a more guided approach to Roving Paragraph Frames. After my first attempt ended in a bit of frustration for all of us, I altered the way I facilitated the activity and used QSSSA (page 66) to scaffold for my new arrival class.

FOR A CLASS WITH MANY EMERGENT WRITERS:

Have students in cooperative groups.

Have pre-printed versions of Roving Paragraph Frames with the following stems:
- Initial sentence frame (For example, "It is important to understand the Bill of Rights because_____.")
- In addition _____
- Finally _____

Give the class the first sentence stem to begin the activity. Use visuals and other sheltered strategies to make the stem comprehensible. Allow native language discussion and use of translation devices. Have students work in groups or pairs and ask them to develop a complete sentence using the frame. Advise them that you will be randomly calling on them.

Have groups give a signal when they have completed the frame.

Randomly call on groups to give their sentences. Teacher scribes sentences on board to model English writing.

Allow each group to offer a sentence and more if time permits.

Chorally read sentences with class and use sheltered strategies to ensure comprehensible input.

Invite students to choose any sentence from the board to be the beginning sentence of their Roving Paragraph Frames. If students have enough writing proficiency, they can use their own words to write their sentence.

Ask the students to stand up with their paper and pencils when they have completed the written sentence.

Tell the students "rove" around the room and find a partner.

Students read their writing to one another. The first person reads the complete sentence, stem and all. The second person listens and then reads his/her complete sentence.

Ask students to write a new sentence that begins with the next stem, "In addition, _____." They can either "borrow or steal" their partner's response if it was different from theirs, or use one from the board. If they have more writing proficiency, they can write their own original sentence.

Once sentence #2 is complete, partners raise their hands or stand back to back. The key here is to incorporate total response signals to indicate to the teacher that the task is complete. Now they are ready to rove again.

Students find new partners, and repeat the entire process with the second partner. It is crucial to instruct students to read everything they have written so far, and for the partner to listen and then read everything that he/she has written so far as well. This validates student responses, and encourages the use of listening and speaking skills. After reading individual sentences, students write a third sentence with the stem "Finally, _____." At this point, each student should have a well-constructed paragraph in hand, complete with transitions and complete thoughts recorded in academic English.

This activity works well at any point in the lesson cycle. It can be used as a warm-up activity, a transition midway through a class period, or as closure to review the day's concepts and learning. Another perk is that you can use this structure to have your students practice other transition words, not just in addition, also, and finally. Sarah Russell, a former English teacher in Reno, NV created a list of signal words that might be useful.

SARAH RUSSELL, A FORMER ENGLISH TEACHER IN RENO, NV CREATED THIS HELPFUL LIST OF SIGNAL WORDS.

ACQUIRING LITERACY

"Class, I saw Gerson yesterday!"

They were excited because they had all been inspired by Gerson's short video when he was only in U.S. schools seven months and had successfully accelerated his English learning (page 65). They had sent questions to Gerson in case I was able to see him.

"Gerson wanted to thank you all for the questions! In addition to his answers he gave about his accent, he also gave me answers to your questions about reading. He told me that he probably read in English for over an hour every day when he was just learning to speak English."

My students exchanged worried glances.

"He did that maybe five days a week. He said that reading a lot is so important. Before he could read a book in English, he used Duolingo. He is still using it. The app helped him get into books. He also loves websites that help you read. He says that he always kept a notebook to write down the words that he wanted to learn. He still has it if any of you would like to have it."

Many hands shot up!

Soon after, the bell rang and we all said goodbye for winter break. I offered for them to take extra books home. They seemed exhausted from the effort necessary for finals this week. Only a couple of students took extra books.

One student, a young man from Colombia came back into the room. This student was in trouble frequently and a few of his teachers told me he was giving no effort in class. He frustrated me as well because he understood so much English but rarely spoke it even with support.

He brought me a cellphone with a very cracked screen and asked me to help him find **www.newsinlevels.com** so he could save it to his phone.

I was so surprised. That was the best Christmas present I could get. A hard-to-reach learner, coming to see me after class, and asking for some reading material at home. – *Carol*

HOW DO I MAKE SENSE OF FOUNDATIONAL LITERACY DEVELOPMENT AT THE SECONDARY LEVEL?

Teachers often ask if it is best to focus on phonemic awareness with students who are learning to read in English. This question is even more significant for our students who are pre-literate or perhaps just emerging with literacy in their native language.

It is unfortunate that most secondary teachers do not have the luxury of foundational literacy training. ESL teachers often get training on second language acquisition, but terms such as "phonological awareness" and "whole language approach" can leave a secondary teacher confused about where to begin. Even our upper elementary teachers are in a position where foundations of literacy may not be in their toolbelt because most of their students are typically partially literate, if not in English, at least in their native language.

Many of our students who are SIFE have literacy in their native language. Some can also read in English. But the reality is that some of these students are not sufficiently literate in any language, so teachers must have at least an awareness of the key concepts of foundational literacy. In most states, this population of students (at Beginning and Intermediate levels of proficiency in English language proficiency in grades 3 and up) must be provided intensive support in acquiring reading and writing skills in English.

Some literacy teachers will tell you that you must focus on phonemic awareness when teaching emergent readers. Other specialists will advocate for the whole language approach as the only way to teach literacy effectively. All of us benefit from an understanding of the principles of these two approaches. The following pages will familiarize you with theories behind teaching reading and writing with a focus on both phonemic awareness and whole language approach and why these practical techniques capitalize on our understanding of how a person learns to read....whether it's in their first language or a new language they are acquiring.

WHAT ARE BEST PRACTICES WITH REGARD TO LITERACY?

ESL teachers must spread themselves across multiple disciplines to help make content comprehensible and develop academic language for ELLs. When students with little or no formal literacy arrive to our schools, it is critical that the ESL teacher understand best practices of literacy instruction and find practical ways to support these emergent readers. In working with students with limited literacy, it helps to become familiar with key ideas that leverage as many of these best practices for literacy development as possible.

BALANCED LITERACY

Whole Language or Phonics? Answer: Both!

Whole Language is the method of teaching reading that emphasizes meaning and strategy instruction. Phonics is a method of teaching reading by connecting sounds with letters. Phonological awareness skills are a prerequisite to phonics instruction. Phonological Awareness is the broad ability to identify and manipulate larger parts of spoken language.

Example: alliteration, rhyme, words, and syllables.

Phonemic Awareness is a subcategory of Phonological Awareness. It is the ability to hear, identify and manipulate the smallest units of sound (called phonemes). Example: Separating the word "map" into three distinct sounds, /m/, /æ/, and /p/.

The goal of a Balanced Literacy approach is to utilize the strongest elements of both whole language and phonics instruction. Some components of a 'balanced literacy' approach are as follows:

read aloud
teacher reads aloud to students while pointing at the words

shared reading
teacher reads aloud modeling reading strategies and provides opportunities for students to read aloud

guided reading
teacher pulls aside small groups of students and has them read aloud to him/her, focusing on developing reading strategies and skills, while other students work independently

independent reading
students read self-selected texts silently for increasing amounts of time

write aloud
teacher creates a model of writing in front of the students while explaining aloud the thought processes behind various elements of high quality writing

shared writing
teacher creates a model of writing in collaboration with the students that becomes an example of high quality student writing

guided writing
teacher pulls aside small groups of students, having them complete writing tasks prompted by intentional questions/stems focused on developing writing strategies and skills, while other students work independently

independent writing
students write on self-selected topics gradually increasing the length and/or quality of their writing

As a secondary ESL teacher, I appreciate the importance of understanding best practices for teaching literacy. I need to know why approaches like these are effective so that we can use our time as wisely as possible. I focus a great deal on shared reading and shared writing in the first semester with more and more time for guided and independent writing as the year progresses.

The approaches above have value for the content teacher as well. If I am a math teacher, my primary goal is to teach math content. But it benefits my entire class if I understand how a student acquires a second language, literacy and academic math language. For example, Marzano and Pickering (2007) assert that a person's knowledge of any topic is encapsulated in the terms he/she knows that are relevant to the topic. If your content area happens to be one that is assessed by standardized tests, you are well aware of the need for literacy with respect to your content. Gone are the days of math assessments that are primarily testing by calculations. **If we understand how a person learns new terms, a new language, and grows in literacy, we will be more effective with our content teaching for all.**

WHAT DO I NEED TO KNOW ABOUT HOW STUDENTS THAT ARE SIFE ACQUIRE LITERACY?

For teachers of students who are SIFE, it is critical to have an understanding of how literacy is acquired, especially in the early stages. We should first have a clear understanding of their capabilities in the realm of literacy. Despite years of gaps in schooling, a student may have some literacy in their native language and even in the target language. Native language literacy is a major advantage for students who are learning to read in their new language. Initial assessments (p.25-31) should be conducted or acquired from your intake staff to determine the student's functional levels of literacy.

Should your SIFE learners have little to no literacy, do not despair. We feel a great deal of concern for these students, but we should in no way feel that their situation is hopeless. Remember that our SIFE students who are pre-literate are not operating at the level of a kindergartner who is learning to read. Older SIFE learners will have acquired more background knowledge than our early childhood students. Our students will bring more experiences to the table, which serve as their funds of knowledge.

Their brains are more developed than younger learners. We have mentioned other things to keep in mind as well. Background knowledge and their ability to understand metacognitive strategies are keys to helping your students remain in a growth mindset. These factors allow a student who is SIFE to learn to read at a more rapid pace than a younger learner. For instance, a SIFE learner has the potential to progress through many grade levels in as little as two years with the right instructional support and study practices in place.

For students who are SIFE to be successful in this realm, they must engage in significant amounts of reading. To foster a productive reading environment, teachers can use practices such as choral reading, free voluntary reading, and the Language Experience Approach.

READING

READ ALOUD / TRACKING PRINT

My students understand the research behind reading daily. This is one of the concrete data correlations I share with them:

VARIATION IN AMOUNT OF INDEPENDENT READING

Independent Reading Minutes Per Day	Words Read Per Year
65.0	4,358,000
21.1	1,823,000
14.2	1,146,000
9.6	622,000
6.5	432,000
4.6	282,000
3.2	200,000
1.3	106,000
0.7	21,000
0.1	8,000
0.0	0

Chart adapted from a study by Anderson, Wilson, and Fielding (1988), as printed in Cunningham & Stanovich, "What Reading Does for the Mind", (1998)

Once I show my students the number of words they will read in a year with just 20 minutes of reading per day, they are much more apt to track print as I read aloud. Although this study is on independent reading, it shows a correlation to number of words read in a year and amount of time spent reading. This type of data helps students see that the more they engage with text, the more words they will acquire.

I often record myself reading a passage so I can circulate the room while the students track the print. We do this in a whole group setting often but the students can soon track print on their own with audio books and web readers. It is important to do as much of this as possible so that our emergent readers begin to get exposure to high frequency words. Tracking while the words are being pronounced by someone else also helps students develop phonological awareness. We need our emergent readers attending to English print from their first day in class. We can hook them as readers even before they can read independently. That will, of course, eventually lead to independent reading.

WHAT IS CHORAL READING?

Choral reading with students who are SIFE is an effective practice. This activity is critical for emergent readers as well as for students who are new to a language. The goal is to expose students to as much print as possible and help them practice pronunciation and fluency. Often the texts we choral read are co-created, that is, we write the text together as a class. Given our students' high need for affirmation and culturally responsive teaching strategies, a shared writing and shared reading approach has been very effective as the beginning steps for English literacy with my students who are SIFE.

We have many goals for our students, but for many students, their perception of how they pronounce words is one of their main concerns when attempting to speak in the target language. So this activity can be beneficial for all students as we are also asking them to have authentic conversations and participate in structured writing activities.

Having my students read aloud in unison

accomplishes a number of other things that are important for older emergent readers as well. The following are some of the goals that are met when we read a selection of text together:

- Affective filter is lowered. Students realize that no one can hear their pronunciation practice if the entire class is reading at once.

- Multiple exposures to high frequency English words in context.

- Language learners are exposed to grammatical structures in the L2.

- Students practice using unfamiliar words in unison before having to use the language on their own.

- Students are invested in the content because many of the texts we read together are co-created with the students.

- Comprehension is increased because the co-created mentor texts provide understanding in the shared writing process, so reading is not a struggle.

This video (**bit.ly/NabilReads**) shows an example of how the strategy helped one student gain enough exposure to English to begin his reading journey. Nabil had no literacy in his primary language. In fact, after a few months in my classroom he still didn't believe he had any literacy in English. But I knew that he had mastered more sight words and more phonemic awareness than he realized. I wrote each student a letter. I was not successful in finding any other high interest text that worked with him. But I knew that Nabil would want to read his letter. I was banking on the fact that if he could master this letter, he would have a piece of text that he could read on his own.

NABIL'S
READING
VIDEO

For an update on his reading, you can watch a video (**Bit.ly/NabilUpdate**) that we filmed a few months later. That first experience was enough to convince Nabil that he had the metacognitive strategies that would help him boost his language and literacy skills. I was very proud when he won a scholarship for high school supplies with a 400 word essay that he wrote with my help and could read independently.

So, what does effective choral reading look like? To have my students choral read with me, I first read the text aloud, making sure to track the text with my finger or pointer, reading each word clearly, and speaking at an appropriate pace. Then the students read aloud with me, while I continue to track the text. To be effective with choral reading, I suggest that you explain the brain-friendliness of verbalizing new words and tracking print. We want our students to understand that the simple act of reading aloud while tracking the text can provide them with more exposure and practice with text and language.

For new selections, I read each sentence first saying "This is what it sounds like…" I model the pronunciation and fluency of the sentence once. The students wait for me to say "Everyone on two. One, two.." and they read in unison. Quick Writes that we create together become anchor charts and also are recorded in their own handwriting. This provides text they are able to read independently for practice on their own. (See "Language Experience Approach," page 82.)

NABIL'S
READING
UPDATE

Whether we are going to read our objectives, a shared writing piece or a math word problem, we want to get the most out of the activity. If we are creating the text, we want to consider what academic language the student will need to be successful. Some of that is scaffolding mortar words such as "in a similar fashion" instead of "like" or "the same as." We consistently focus on modeling appropriate use of academic language throughout the school year.

If we are reading a mentor text, I chunk the selection and identify any language that could be confusing for the student. Reading aloud with the student provides the teacher with an opportunity to "think aloud" and problem solve unfamiliar words so as to make these strategies visible to the learner. Teachers can model strategies such as skipping words, decoding strategies, and monitoring for meaning.

WHAT ABOUT READING IN CONTENT AREA CLASSES?

It's very helpful to understand the basic principles of balanced literacy to realize what is working in our favor when we do reading and writing activities in ESL or content classes. ESL teachers of emergent readers should track progress of phonological awareness, fluency, concepts of print and other literacy competencies to help students close their specific gaps. Content teachers are tracking progress of content knowledge while supporting literacy and language to the extent possible.

I would reiterate here that literacy levels affect our ability to learn any content subject in today's secondary classroom. If a science teacher wants to support the literacy of her students who are SIFE, she may take opportunities to chorally read objectives, sentence frames and vocabulary with the class. Also consider what this does for your science students who are on level for language and literacy. A focus on objectives is said to have a significant impact on student achievement (Marzano et al., 2001). While we may not have time to routinely stop our

math class to teach reading strategies, it would benefit all learners to partake in some of the reading activities that are practical and beneficial for all learners.

Some examples of high-impact, practical techniques include:

- Chorally reading of learning and language objectives.

- Posting a specific language objective that provides the English that students need to accomplish the content objective.

- Chorally reading key vocabulary or new vocabulary in the objectives.

- Asking students to analyze objectives and discuss what they think they mean.

- Structured conversations with pre-taught key vocabulary.

- Chorally reading sentence frames that support content objectives.

- Providing reading partners where listener is responsible for summarizing key ideas and reader is modeling fluency.

FREE VOLUNTARY READING

Free Voluntary Reading (FVR) is a research-based and effective method for rapidly developing literacy. Instructional gaps experienced by students who are SIFE often place them three or more grade levels behind their peers of the same age. This literacy gap is sometimes even wider because of low or non-existent literacy in the students' primary or native language.

How do we help students who are SIFE fill this gap? Getting students hooked on reading is a crucial component in building literacy skills and encouraging reading, both inside and outside of class. This means students are excited not only about reading itself, but what they are reading.

As students are first gaining literacy, it is important to offer options during FVR time that are accessible to emergent readers. See page 55 for ideas and helpful resources.

As teachers, our goal is to provide students with engaging text that is high-interest to "hook" our students, but is at a reading level commensurate with the students' own reading abilities.

FVR involves ESL/Language Arts teachers developing a program in which students have structured time to engage in reading self-selected texts. There are a variety of approaches to engaging students in self-selected reading. The approach advocated here is based on the collected research of Robert Marzano in his book, *Building Academic Background Knowledge for Academic Achievement: Research on What Works in Schools* (2004). FVR programs have been demonstrated to be one of the most powerful ways to increase students' language development in the target language.

Examples

Some resources for Free Voluntary Reading can be found in:

Free Voluntary Reading
Stephen Krashen (2011)

The Book Whisperer: Awakening the Inner Reader in Every Child
Donalyn Miller (2009)

The SSR Handbook: How to Organize and Manage a Sustained Silent Reading Program
Janice Pilgreen (2000)

Building Student Literacy Through Sustained Silent Reading – Steve Gardiner (2005)

DIRECTIONS

1. Students identify topics that interest them.
Use tools such as student surveys, classroom conversations, individual conversations with students, and brainstorming to discover topics that students find interesting.

2. Students find reading materials associated with topics of interest.
Help students find books of interest by collaborating with the librarian, developing your own personal library, and explaining to students how to find books online and at local libraries. It is your responsibility to help the student identify reading material of interest. The books can be below grade level or above grade level. If possible, try to locate books or articles featuring the student's home country or culture to encourage interest/engagement. The most important element is that the student finds and engages in reading the texts. Books in English or the native language that might be interesting to beginning adolescent readers can be found through sources such as High Noon Publishers.

3. Teachers give students uninterrupted time to read.
You must provide class time, often in intervals of 20 minutes or more, in order for students to actively engage in reading texts they find interesting. Sometimes students may not be able to read silently for 20 minutes when you begin this process; you may need to begin at five minute intervals and gradually increase the time to up to 60 minutes of sustained silent reading.

4. Students write or do something else associated with what they have read.
In order for students to continue to maintain an interest in reading, this step must not seem like busywork or be unpleasant to students. Students with emergent literacy skills can draw pictures or take simple notes about their books, or maintain reading logs. They can write short reflections or share orally with another student.

5. Students interact with the information they have gained through reading.
Students need to share what they are learning and experiencing through the books they read with the other students in the class. This can take on a variety of formats. One great online resource is called "75 Ways to Share a Book" by Suzanne Barchers. It includes suggestions such as writing about it to a friend, creating a new ending for it, writing a biography of one of the characters, persuading a small group from the class to read it or not read it, describing the main character in 64 words, etc.

It is extremely important for reading and the activities associated with Free Voluntary Reading to remain engaging and compelling. If students view the sharing of books as boring, you will accomplish the opposite of what you intend to do through the creation and implementation of an FVR program.

LEA: LANGUAGE EXPERIENCE APPROACH

As we've now learned, the affective filter plays a critical role in second language acquisition. Students who are SIFE need a safe and supportive language learning environment to be able to safely practice their developing English language skills. One of the most effective research-based strategies for structuring this environment while building a solid foundation for literacy is called the Language Experience Approach (LEA). The interactive nature of LEA, the shared experiences of classmates, and the error-correcting free environment of LEA makes it such a success for younger early or pre-literacy learners. Given the fact that our students who are SIFE are more often than not in this same category, it is no surprise that the success of LEA with younger learners transfers to success with SIFE and other under-schooled learners. It is possible that both categories of learners have not yet attained solid English literacy skills, and do not fully understand the processes of reading and writing. The connection between social skills (what is heard and what is spoken) to academic literacy skills (reading and writing) has yet to be solidified.

What may set students who are SIFE apart from younger, pre-literate learners, is the motivation behind the critical need to develop oral and literacy skills in the English language. As Nessel and Dixon (2008) write, "their native language is no longer adequate for their daily needs or for the more complex language requirements of school…" (page 7). They may have to learn a new system of sounds (phonology) and symbols (orthography) that could be radically different from that of their native language. This poses increased challenges for older learners, as their brains attempt to negotiate meaning and discrimination of new and unfamiliar sounds, and then make an attempt to reproduce them. The affective filter increases if this reproduction is done in an unwelcoming environment, alone, with un-supporting peers, or those lacking empathy. An environment that is supportive of an ELL making mistakes and not worrying about errors being corrected in front of others is not only beneficial but essential.

When preparing the classroom setting to take part in LEA, it is important to encourage the communication to be as natural as possible, and for the topic chosen for the activity to be relevant and encouraging to all students as a shared classroom experience. The key for a successful LEA is to use students own vocabulary, language patterns, and shared experiences to create texts for reading and to make the reading process meaningful and enjoyable (Nessel and Dixon (2008).

1. Speaking & Listening
2. Composing (Oral)
3. Listening & Reading
4. Developing Reading/Word Recognition
5. Writing

Step 1: Discuss a shared experience, such as a field trip or classroom project.

Step 2: As students discuss the experience in their own words, the teacher reframes their statements, recording their thoughts on chart paper for all students to see. At this point, students are connecting oral to written language by seeing their own thoughts and words recorded on paper.

Step 3: Once constructed, the teacher reads the text out loud to the students, modeling the sounds of the language with expression. Then with the teacher's help, students practice reading the text several times.

Step 4: The teacher guides the students in recognizing specific words and aids in their development of reading skills such as determining meaning from context, phonics, and structures of the language.

Step 5: Students then use the shared text as a springboard for writing original compositions.

WHY LEA IS BENEFICIAL FOR STUDENTS THAT ARE SIFE

Listening: Through encouraging multiple students in speaking and orally expressing their thoughts and ideas, students will be practicing their listening skills. If native English speakers are present, this provides a great opportunity for students who are SIFE to listen to models of native-English sounds and structures that they can later mimic in their practice. Additionally, as students listen to statements made both by their peers and with the guidance of the teacher, the process of hearing the spoken word being dictated into written text by the teacher is solidifying the literacy connection.

Speaking: Because of their common, shared experience, students are naturally inclined to be comfortable, engaged, and enthusiastic about sharing their thoughts on a topic when creating a collaborative written account. This increases the chance of a stress-free environment that mimics a real-life communication situation, which is an ideal setting for practicing speaking in a new language. The lower the anxiety, the more students will be willing to take risks and practice with vocabulary and expressions that are new to them. Also, the lower the affective filter, the greater chances of language output being produced.

Reading: In addition to reading the words and sentences that are being dictated for the students, SIFE learners in the classroom have multiple exposures to the text, both that day and in lessons and days to follow.

After the shared text is created, students first read along as the teacher is reading the text out loud, and then students practice reading individually multiple times. Multiple readings help build the sight vocabulary and reading fluency.

Texts such as those created in the LEA process are highly meaningful and oftentimes culturally relevant to the students in the classroom, and thus increasing engagement as well as enjoyment of the reading process.

Writing: As reading skills grow, the development of reading will positively transfer to the students' abilities as writers, as students who are SIFE experience the connection between spoken word and written language. Having created a shared composition, students gain increased confidence in experimenting with the creation of original writing compositions.

LEA is truly a precursor to the more formal writing process that is learned in Language Arts classrooms, and through this approach students who are SIFE gain exposure to the concepts of brainstorming and pre-writing, drafting, revising, editing, and then finally publishing.

LANGUAGE EXPERIENCE APPROACH WITH ENGLISH LANGUAGE LEARNERS:

Introduce reading materials that are culturally relevant.

Connect reading with student's background knowledge and experiences.

Replace discrete skill exercises and drills with many opportunities to read.

Provide opportunities for silent reading (in student's first language or English).

Read aloud frequently to students so that they become familiar with the sounds and structures of written language.

Read aloud while students have access to the text to facilitate connecting oral and written modalities.

Recognize that first and second language growth increased with abundant reading and writing.

LEA is grounded in these specific strategies stated in a 2006 position paper on English language learning by NCTE.

Writing is a process. The word process attaches proper significance to the way writing happens, the way writing has always happened.

- Joyce Armstrong Carroll and Edward E. Wilson, Acts of Teaching, 2008

WRITING

Of the four language domains, writing has always been the most difficult for me to support with learners who are SIFE. I quickly realized what would work to get reading off the ground: shared reading and daily choral reading/tracking print was leading to independence with my students who were SIFE. But writing was a different story. I made a point to visit Kindergarten classrooms to see what techniques they used to grow emergent writers. I began implementing shared writing activities and regular writing practice with frames, but this was nowhere near grade-level.

Everything changed when the YMCA International offered scholarships to 8th grade refugee students. Each scholarship was awarded based on a 250+ word essay. I thought this was some kind of joke. How in the world were my under-schooled students, new to English, supposed to be able to write a personal essay?

Again, shame on me for my low expectations. The prompt was "Tell the similarities and differences between your country and the U.S.A. Also explain any advice you would give to a new student from your country." This seemed a daunting task. I am ashamed to say that we almost didn't attempt it. But I wanted them to have this opportunity, and I knew I just needed a way for them to express their own ideas in writing.

We started with a Venn Diagram. Students discussed and recorded things that were the same and different about their lives then and now. For homework, I assigned them the task of thinking through the advice they would give a new student. Many got help from friends and siblings and we were able to complete the brainstorming sheet for the 12 eighth graders who wanted to participate.

At that point, we were able to use this information to fill in paragraph frames that would tell their unique stories. I helped with the English, but the students were the ones that decided to do things like change the order of paragraphs, tell more about a particular detail, and cut out sentences that didn't sound right. They were revising! What an amazing thing to see. These students were absolutely hitting grade-level writing standards that called for prewriting, draft, revision, voice, and even publishing with technology. Much of the drafting and revising was done with my support or that of a volunteer. But these types of collaborations are encouraged in any good writer's workshop. We were thrilled when seven of my students won scholarships from the YMCA.

Since this project, my eyes have been opened to many grade-level ELAR standards that can be taught and mastered by students who are gaining literacy and language. This activity exemplifies what I know to be true about writing. As a certified Abydos writing trainer, I know that teaching writing is not so much about the final product but about teaching the process of writing. This is true for every student. For more on Abydos Learning, visit **www.abydoslearning.org**. Watch this short video to see my students engaged in the YMCA scholarship writing opportunity: **bit.ly/NabilUpdate**. For more on the YMCA International programs, visit **www.ymca.int**. – *Carol*

THE WRITING PROCESS
Adapted from Abydos/New Jersey Writing Project

STAGE OF THE WRITING PROCESS	DESCRIPTION OF STAGE	HOW THE SIFE LEARNER IS ENGAGED
Pre-Writing	This is the work we do before writing. It can be anything that gets kids thinking. Examples of activities include illustrating, acting out, listing ideas, labeling things, creating something, free writing, brainstorming and many more.	Many of these can be done by any student at any language or literacy level. Illustrating in response to writing is worthwhile for any student at any grade level as a form of pre-writing. According to Carroll and Wilson in *Acts of Teaching* (2008), drawing is a powerful way of writing and different from drawing as an art form. Student examples, retellings of their drawings and writing connections are more evidence that drawings are not just representational. Drawings can be powerful tools that lead to more exploration and discovery.
Writing	Begins with rough draft. A focus on genre will support student writers to organize their papers. According to Carroll and Wilson in *Acts of Teaching* (2008), students must consume a variety of pieces with different genre and internalize those choices. Only then can they take what they want to say and decide how they will say it with the form that best allows them to express themselves.	Native language writing is acceptable here. The goal is to get thoughts out in a simple draft reflecting their ideas. Many students struggle with getting from pre-writing to the first draft. SIFE students, like all writing students, can read different genres of literature to help them make choices about how they want to express their ideas. Do they want to write a letter, a fictional story or a personal essay? They are able to make these choices and then, depending on their language and writing abilities, sentence or paragraph frames may be of great help. For a pre-literate student, this can be done orally and through shared writing as they gain more literacy.

STAGE OF THE WRITING PROCESS	DESCRIPTION OF STAGE	HOW THE SIFE LEARNER IS ENGAGED
Revising/ Reformulation/ Editing	According to Carroll and Wilson, Revising for Grammar is different from Correcting. (Correcting deals with distractions that might affect the reader. Revising, on the other hand, has more to do with distractions that could affect the writer's meaning.) This is really multiple stages that deal with revising and changing their writing at the word, sentence, and paragraph level. See *Acts of Teaching* by Carroll and Wilson (2008) for detailed descriptions and activities that help grow writers and guide students through the writing process.	This stage can seem overwhelming because we know that grammar, spelling, and conventions play a role in our revising. However, every learner can internalize concepts about the grammatical structures of their second language. Students who are SIFE are constantly doing this at their level of proficiency. Teachers can address language proficiency goals with the revising process. Peer conferences and teacher-student conferences can scaffold for the English grammar some ELLs may need to acquire. Instead of thinking of this process as too complex for our SIFE students, it could be seen as an excellent opportunity to help them internalize grammatical structures in context with text that is highly meaningful to them.
Publishing	There are a variety of ways to publish the writing of our students. Examples include Author's Chair, Read-Around, Book-Making, publishing to the internet or the walls of our school hallways.	All kids love to publish. We can have a fun place with glitter and colored paper. We can also just offer time for students to type out their writing in Google docs. Many students benefit from typing their hand-written essays for practice with technology and most importantly, pride in their work.

SCAFFOLDED PARAGRAPH FRAMES

We only meet two or three times per week for 90 minutes. So we usually create mentor texts as a shared quick write. We have a class discussion, and I give the students sentence frames to turn and talk. I allow native language discussion. Then I randomly call on students to answer with the English frame.

Sometimes I get "One thing I noticed was que el hombre está enojado." So we quickly recast "...he was mad? Okay, that sounds like "One thing I noticed was that he was mad. Everyone say that..."

Everyone repeats the sentence, and meanwhile I am adding the thought to our brainstorming on the whiteboard. Soon, we have enough input from students that I am able to model a think aloud and quick write. I usually ask the students to discuss what a good first or last sentence would be. They are copying the paragraph as I am writing. Everyone chorally reads this. It is now a mentor text. We sometimes revise these as another activity.

– Carol

Providing sentence stems and paragraph frames is a key strategy to use in scaffolding writing opportunities for all English language learners, especially students who are SIFE. Stems and frames not only support language structures, but can help provide emergent writers with a springboard for expressing their thoughts in complete sentences.

In my classroom, we've used the following sentence frames that lead to the students writing a complete paragraph. This was an authentic experience for my students, for these questions were asked by a reporter from our school newspaper.

Your Name: _____

QUESTIONS FOR THE ORACLE
NEWSPAPER REPORTER

(Your answers will be turned into a paragraph
that should include more elaboration.)

1) Which country were you originally from?
   I was originally from _____.

2) Did you live in any other countries before you came to the U.S?
   I first lived in _____ and then _____ before I came to the U.S.
   OR: I have never lived in any other country.

3) When did you move to the U.S?
   I moved to the U.S. in _____.

4) Why did you or your family decide to move to the U.S.?
   I (my family) moved here because _____ .

5) Describe your daily life, your daily schedule before you came to the U.S.
   On most days I would first _____. Then I would _____.
   Later I would _____ and finally I would _____.

6) What were some similarities and differences than your life now?
   One thing that is the same about my country and the U.S. is that _____.
   (Another thing that is the same is _____.) However there are many differences. One key
   difference is _____. Another…..

7) How did you learn English, and what motivated you to do so?
   I learned English by _____. I also _____
   Another thing I do is _____. I think _____….

8) What have you liked about your life in the U.S. so far?
   Something I really like about my life in the U.S. is _____.

9) Are there any things that surprised you when you first moved here?
   Something that really surprised me at first was _____.
   Is there anything you miss from your life before the U.S.?
   I really miss _____ .

10) Academically speaking, which country do you think challenges you more- the U.S., or your country?
   _____ is much harder for the subject of _____.
   I think this is because _____ .

WRITING IN CONTENT AREAS

A recent immigrant can do quite a lot of writing the day they arrive in the country. They must engage in the production of English writing immediately and there are ways to support this, which benefit the entire class.

Earlier in this book I mentioned a master teacher, Joseph Maurer (see page 45). Maurer's math class was an excellent example of how writing and producing language in content areas can boost achievement of all learners. The students in Maurer's classroom have math journals that are filled with reflective writing about their math learning. The support for second language acquisition is critical for the ELLs in that classroom but it is also an important practice for all of his students. My own son, who is not an ELL, was in Mr. Maurer's algebra class. Anthony would tell me that Maurer was a great math teacher and that he let the students talk about math a lot. I noticed that his homework included less calculations and more writing reflection with stems such as "I solved this problem by…" or "I noticed…"

Even an unschooled, second language learner is able to list, label and copy from day one as they practice forming English letters and words. We can't wait for the ELL to have advanced levels of English writing ability to expect writing in content areas. We must provide support with sheltered instruction such as sentence frames and opportunities for oral language practice the day they arrive in our classrooms.

Writing in the math classroom is a critical support for the ELLs in Joseph Maurer's math class (see page 45). But it is definitely benefiting every learner in that content classroom.

In his book, *Clearing the Way: Working with Teenage Writers,* Romano (1987) stresses that content teachers outside of language arts do not need to teach writing, but they should all realize that writing has us using language-and that is what makes us think.

- Content area teachers can use writing for more than assessing what students have learned. They can have students write to learn.

- Writing is thinking on paper. If we trust that a child must process ideas to be reflective about them, and then to write about them, it is easy to see the value in writing about any subject.

- Writing begins with pre-writing. Many pre-writing activities are perfect to engage our newcomers in higher order thinking skills about content subject. These activities can be used to build background knowledge for the class or after a task as an exit ticket. A newcomer's writing may not look the same as other students, but their reflections and expression are critical nonetheless.

- Teachers trained in the writing process will have many pre-writing strategies to draw from. Some examples of pre-writing strategies include Orally Describing/Listing/Rephrasing, Sentence Frames, Free Writing, Native Language Writing, Brainstorming, Illustrating, and Story-boarding.

RESOURCES AND COMMUNITY PARTNERS

RESOURCES FOR CONTINUED GROWTH

If you'd like to become more proficient with technology for your classroom, we recommend the book *ELL Frontiers, Using Technology to Enhance Instruction of English Learners* by Parris, Estrada and Honigsfeld (2016).

TWITTER

It is important to collaborate with and learn from other professionals with similar goals. Teachers of English learners would benefit from following innovative professionals on Twitter such as Tan Hyunh (@TanELLclassroom) and Larry Ferlazzo (@LarryFerlazzo). Both of these educators publish excellent resources for teachers of new ELLs. You can also follow my Twitter account @MsSalvaC as I try to regularly share what is working for my students who are SIFE.

You can also grow your Professional Learning Network with many contributing ELL educators by visiting Twitter and searching these popular hashtags: #ELLChat, #ChatESL, #Katyool.

WRITING TRAINING

The Abydos writing institute is recommended for every language arts teacher. The training is typically conducted as an institute where teachers have the opportunity to experience research-based teaching practices to implement in their classrooms. For more information, see **www.abydoslearning.org**

COMMUNITY PARTNERS

Many school districts and educational institutions have formed partnerships with cultural community organizations, religious organizations, and university student groups that are familiar with the culture and language of students who are SIFE. These groups can be an invaluable resource in providing translation and explanations of campus culture, acting as role models, and communicating with parents. Be open to what is available where you are. The same resources that are available in one city might not be available in another. It is impressive how many people are willing to come and help students who are SIFE, as soon as teachers are willing to ask. We are grateful to those organizations and individuals who have stepped up to the plate and helped our students.

Model Example of a Community Partner

No Pass, No Play is an important regulation that normally serves to motivate athletes that might fall behind in studies otherwise. Unfortunately, it is a Catch-22 for our students who are SIFE. Being new to the country, they can desperately use the advantages of team sports. Their often off-level academic skills, however, prohibit them from participating until they close their achievement gaps.

Family Point is a community outreach center in our neighborhood that we did not learn about until late in the second semester. We were grateful to Coach Stribling and Ms. Hruzak, their education coordinator. This center partners with many organizations in Houston to offer our families a wide variety of support. One of their programs that has made an incredible difference for our students that are SIFE is their track team. At the date of publication of this book, several of our students are running for the Family Point Speed Track Team. A fun fact is that Francies and his brother Emmanuel actually qualified for the AAU National Junior Olympics through the team. Over 14,000 athletes competed and our students were among the top performers. Francies finished 17th and Emmanuel was 14th in the nation for their events. They were both new to the sport of track. Imagine what they'll do with a bit more training!

Family Point also provides free ESL and GED classes for older siblings and parents. They provide programs like "Brighter Bites" (that offers healthy groceries and recipes), a community library, free internet, computer and printing services, as well as a host of other support programs for our families. Volunteers have come to us through Family Point for which we are very grateful. Family Point even organized and ran a successful ESL summer school program for our refugee students which included meals and transportation.

Example of Community Volunteers

We are grateful to Ms. Morford, one of our PTA members, who mobilized a large number of missionaries from the Mormon Church to come to the middle school regularly for ESL support lessons.

Special thanks to our Stratford High PTSA president, Ms. Seltzman who also communicated with PTSA members and mobilized

several volunteers to visit my NELD class on a regular basis. Other volunteers such as G. Agosto, A. Haddon and L. Maple are stellar examples of people who will spend their time to better their community and support our newest students. We were overwhelmed by the support when we finally got organized enough to receive it.

Lesson learned: go out into the community and find out what is available to your students and their families.

COMMUNITY PARTNERS

Libraries
Local libraries may provide collections for older students gaining literacy. They also often have supportive resources for our families and students such as internet, tutoring, classes and other community engagement services.

Outreach Centers -
Check **www.outreachcenters.net** for centers in your area. Also check with your district's social worker to find out about any assistance for your residents. Family Point Resources offers many services to students and families in our area.

YMCA International
Community-focused nonprofit with programs & services for all ages.

Refugee resettlement organizations
Become familiar with services provided by the organizations that have resettled families to your area. Funding is sometimes available for tutoring and academic support as well as family support.

School PTA & community volunteers
Our community members started flooding in when we showed them how easy it is to make an impact as a volunteer.
(Example: **bit.ly/LanguageVolunteers**)

School student organizations
World Affairs Club and National Honor Society had students who were happy to help us with peer-tutoring after school. Our school newspaper did a story on our students in a positive light. This honored our students and also lead to a great writing assignment.

Churches/religious organizations
Our area churches had many programs in place for our students and their families. ESL classes, Free GED classes and meal programs are a few examples.

Government Education Service Centers
The Department of Education offers many programs to support teachers and families. GED classes for family members and ESL classes may be offered at no charge. Also look for Educator network groups for SIFE and Newcomer teachers.

School district/central office support
Look for ways to partner with your district support staff or teachers at other campuses to share curriculum and ideas.

Athletic coaches
Coaches are important allies to help our struggling students stay motivated. They often know of community leagues that may be appropriate for the student and their families for involvement in organized sports.

Authors
Rarely will an author turn you down if you ask for them to communicate with your students. They can respond to letters from your students, they can Skype with your class, and some are happy to visit for story-telling and read-alouds. Be sure to prepare questions and practice prior to visit!
(Example: **bit.ly/AuthorVisitPrep**)

Small business owners
Entrepreneurship is a great part of the American Dream. There are business owners all around you and they may be willing to interact with your students as part of a writing or project assignment. They could respond to letters or emails, Skype, or visit with your class. Be sure to prepare questions and practice prior to visit!
(Example: **bit.ly/RestaurantVisit**)

Artists/fine arts organizations
Young Audiences of Houston helped us find funding for an African dance program after school. Research Arts organizations in your area to see if they offer outreach.
(Example: **bit.ly/AfricanDanceExample**)

University student organizations
Teacher organizations and other university student groups may want to offer time to support your learners. Contact local institutions.

Volunteer organizations
Many groups specifically work to help newcomers in their new land.
(Example: **www.pairhouston.org**)

Adult education

Programs such as The Plaza Comunitarias program in Texas's Plano ISD offers offers GED classes and also high school diploma programs with Spanish as the language of instruction. School districts can obtain resources to offer this type of program by entering into an agreement with Mexico. With 47 consulates (**www.sre.gob.mx/acerca/directorio/consulados/dirconsulados.htm**) across the United States, school districts can contact consulate personnel to assist with their agreement. When the agreement is signed, the Mexican agency provides each Plaza Comunitaria with textbooks, online curriculum, videos, CDs and rights to duplicate curriculum materials.

Crowdfunding organizations

Pledgecents.com is one of the crowdfunding platforms that were a tremendous help to us for funding study trips and supplies. Here is one example: **bit.ly/PCSalvaBlog**

WEBSITES

**State Educational Service Centers/
Departments of Education**

 **U.S. Department
of Education
Newcomer Toolkit**

 CAL: Newcomer resources

*Welcome to the United States:
 A Guidebook for Refugees*

 *Welcome to the United States:
Refugee Guide to Resettlement*

 *Cultural Orientation
Resource Center
(website sponsored by CAL)*

 **Seidlitz Education,
Texas Student
Refugee Framework**

 **UNHCR,
The UN Refugee
Agency**

 **Multilinguals
Forward**

 **Immigrant
Connections: The U.S.
Refugee School Impact
Program**

 **MALP: The Mutually
Adaptive Learning
Program**

 **The SIFE
Equity Project**

 **Carol Salva's Blog
bit.ly/SalvaBlog**

SOURCES

Brotherton, S., & Williams, C. (2002). Interactive writing instruction in a first grade title I literacy program. *Journal of Reading Education, 27*(3), 8-19.

Carr, N. G. (2011). *The shallows: What the internet is doing to our brains.* New York, NY: W.W. Norton.

Carroll, J. A., & Wilson, E. E. (2008). *Acts of teaching: How to teach writing: A text, a reader, a narrative.* Portsmouth, NH: Heinemann.

Csíkszentmihályi, M. (2008). *Flow: The psychology of optimal experience.* New York, NY: Harper & Row.

Cunningham, A. E., & Stanovich, K. E. (1998). What reading does for the mind. *American Educator/American Federation of Teachers, (Spring/Summer).* Retrieved March 13, 2017, from https://www.aft.org/sites/default/files/periodicals/cunningham.pdf

Dweck, C. S. (2008). *Mindset: The new psychology of success.* New York, NY: Ballantine Books.

Dweck, C. (2015). Carol Dweck revisits the 'growth mindset.' *Education Week,* 35(5), 20-4.

Duckworth, A. (2016). *Grit: The power of passion and perseverance.* New York, NY: Scribner.

Echevarria, J., Vogt, M.E. & Short, D. (2008). *Making content comprehensible for English language learners: The SIOP® model, (3rd ed.).* Boston, MA: Allyn & Bacon.

Gay, G. (2010). *Culturally responsive teaching: Theory, research, and practice.* New York, NY: Teachers College.

Healy, J. M. (1999). *Endangered minds: Why children don't think - and what we can do about it.* New York, NY: Simon & Schuster.

Krashen, S. D. (1985). *The input hypothesis: Issues and implications.* New York, NY: Addison-Wesley Longman, Ltd.

Krashen, S. D. (2011). *Free voluntary reading.* Santa Barbara, CA: Libraries Unlimited, ABC-CLIO, LLC.

Krashen, S.D., & Terrell, T.D. (1983). *The natural approach: Language acquisition in the classroom.* London: Prentice Hall Europe.

Marzano, R. J. (2004). *Building background knowledge for academic achievement: Research on what works in schools.* Alexandria, VA: Association for Supervision and Curriculum Development.

Marzano, R. J., & Pickering, D. J. (2007). *Building academic vocabulary: Teacher's manual.* Alexandria, VA: Association for Supervision and Curriculum Development.

Marzano, R. J., Pickering, D., & Pollock, J. E. (2001). *Classroom instruction that works: Research-based strategies for increasing student achievement.* Alexandria, VA: Association for Supervision and Curriculum Development.

Menken, K., & Kleyn, T. (2010). The long-term impact of subtractive schooling in the educational experiences of secondary English language learners. *International Journal of Bilingual Education and Bilingualism, 13*(4), 399-417.

Nessel, D. D., & Dixon, C. N. (2008). *Using the language experience approach with English language learners: Strategies for engaging students and developing literacy.* Thousand Oaks, CA: Corwin Press.

Parris, H., Estrada, L., & Honigsfeld, A. M. (2016). *ELL frontiers: Using technology to enhance instruction for English learners.* Thousand Oaks, CA: Corwin Press.

Romano, T. (1987). *Clearing the way: Working with teenage writers.* Portsmouth, NH: Heinemann Educational.

Seidlitz, J. (2011). *Sheltered instruction plus: A comprehensive plan for successfully teaching English language learners.* San Clemente, CA: Canter Press.

Seidlitz, J., & Kenfield, K. (2011). *38 great academic language builders: Activities for math, science, social studies, language arts...and just about everything else.* San Clemente, CA: Canter Press.

Seidlitz J., & Perryman, B. (2011). *7 Steps to a language-rich interactive classroom: Research-based strategies for engaging all students.* San Clemente, CA: Canter Press.

Seidlitz, J., Base, M., Lara, M., & Smith, H. (2016). *ELLS in Texas: What teachers need to know (2nd ed.).* San Clemente, CA: Canter Press.

WIDA Focus on SLIFE: *Students with Limited or Interrupted Formal Education.* (May, 2015). Retrieved March 13, 2017 from: http://www.njtesol-njbe.org/handouts15/ WIDA_Focus_on_SLIFE.pdf

Seidlitz, J., & Obamehenti, F. (2013). *Texas student refugee framework: A collaborative approach.* San Clemente, CA: Canter Press.

CAROL SALVA is a current Newcomer Teacher at Stratford High School in Houston, Texas. She is also an educational consultant with Seidlitz Education. Carol was named Spring Branch ISD's District Teacher of the Year in 2009. She is a certified writing trainer for Abydos Learning as well as a former Bilingual and Special Education teacher. Carol specializes in using research-based strategies to teach grade-level content to unschooled/under-schooled language learners. Carol Salva holds a Master's degree in Educational Administration with a Principal Certification.

ANNA MATIS is a writer and consultant for Seidlitz Education. Her love of language learning stems from childhood experiences as an immigrant and ESL student from Budapest, Hungary. Proficient in multiple languages, she is passionate about second language acquisition for all ages, sheltered instruction strategies, heritage language learning, and long-term ELL research. Anna has lead professional development at the state and national level, coached teachers in ESL strategies, and created instructional products for both teachers and administrators working with ESL students.

SEIDLITZ EDUCATION · BOOK ORDER FORM

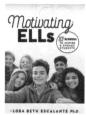

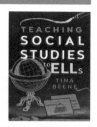

TITLE	PRICE	QTY	TOTAL$
38 Great Academic Language Builders	$24.95		
7 Pasos para crear un aula interactiva y rica en lenguaje SPANISH	$29.95		
7 Steps to a Language-Rich Interactive Classroom	$29.95		
7 Steps To a Language-Rich, Interactive Foreign Language Classroom	$32.95		
Boosting Achievement: Reaching Students with Interrupted or Minimal Education	$26.95		
Content Review & Practice for the TX ESL 154	$39.95		
Content Review & Practice for the TX Bilingual 164	$39.95		
Content Review & Practice for the TX Spanish 190	$39.95		
Diverse Learner Flip Book	$26.95		
ELLs in Texas: What Teachers Need to Know 2ND ED.	$34.95		
ELs in Texas: What School Leaders Need to Know 3RD ED.	$34.95		
ELPS Flip Book	$19.95		
English/Spanish Linguistic and Academic Connections	$29.95		
Mi Cuaderno de Dictado SPANISH	$7.95		
Motivating ELLs: 27 Activities to Inspire & Engage Students	$26.95		
COLUMN 1 TOTAL $			

TITLE	PRICE	QTY	TOTAL$
Navigating the ELPS: Using the Standards to Improve Instruction for English Learners	$24.95		
Navigating the ELPS: Math 2ND EDITION	$29.95		
Navigating the ELPS: Science	$29.95		
Navigating the ELPS: Social Studies	$29.95		
Navigating the ELPS: Language Arts and Reading	$34.95		
Optimizando el desarrollo de la lectoescritura SPANISH	$39.95		
Pathways to Greatness for ELL Newcomers: A Comprehensive Guide for Schools & Teachers	$32.95		
Reading & Writing with English Learners	$29.95		
RTI for ELLs Fold-Out	$16.95		
Sheltered Instruction in Texas: Second Language Acquisition Methods for Teachers of ELs	$29.95		
Talk Read Talk Write: A Practical Routine for Learning in All Content Areas K-12 2ND ED.	$32.95		
Teaching Social Studies to ELLs	$24.95		
Teaching Science to English Learners	$24.95		
¡Toma la Palabra! SPANISH	$32.95		
Vocabulary Now! 44 Strategies All Teachers Can Use	$29.95		
COLUMN 2 TOTAL $			

Pricing, specifications, and availability subject to change without notice.

COLUMN 1+2	$
DISCOUNT	$
SHIPPING	$
TAX	$
TOTAL	$

SHIPPING 9% of order total, minimum $14.95
5-7 business days to ship. If needed sooner please call for rates.
TAX EXEMPT? please fax a copy of your certificate along with order.

HOW TO ORDER

PHONE (210) 315-7119 | ONLINE at **www.seidlitzeducation.com**

FAX completed form with payment info to **(949) 200-4384**

NAME

SHIPPING ADDRESS   CITY   STATE, ZIP

PHONE NUMBER   EMAIL ADDRESS

TO ORDER BY FAX
to **(949) 200-4384**
please complete
credit card info *or*
attach purchase order

☐ Visa ☐ MasterCard ☐ Discover ☐ AMEX

CARD #   EXPIRES
                          mm/yyyy
SIGNATURE   CVV
                      3- or 4- digit code

☐ **Purchase Order attached**
please make
P.O. out to
Seidlitz Education

For information about Seidlitz Education products
and professional development, please contact us at

(210) 315-7119 | kathy@johnseidlitz.com
56 Via Regalo, San Clemente, CA 92673
www.seidlitzeducation.com

Giving kids the
gift of **academic
language.**™

REV050321

Three ways to order

- **FAX** completed order form with payment information to **(949) 200-4384**
- **PHONE** order information to **(210) 315-7119**
- **ORDER ONLINE** at **www.seidlitzeducation.com**

Pricing, specifications, and availability subject to change without notice.

TITLE	Price	QTY	TOTAL $
NEW! *Instead Of I Don't Know* Poster For the LOTE Classroom 24" x 36"			
☐ LOTE FRENCH	$9.95		
☐ LOTE SPANISH	$9.95		
☐ LOTE GERMAN	$9.95		
☐ LOTE ARABIC	$9.95		
☐ LOTE CHINESE	$9.95		
		TOTAL $	

TITLE	Price	QTY	TOTAL $
Instead Of I Don't Know Poster, 24" x 36"			
☐ Elementary ENGLISH	$9.95		
☐ Secondary ENGLISH	$9.95		
20 pack *Instead Of I Don't Know* Posters, 11" x 17"			
☐ Elementary ENGLISH	$40.00		
☐ Secondary ENGLISH	$40.00		
Instead Of I Don't Know Poster, 24" x 36" Elementary SPANISH	$9.95		
20 pack *Instead Of I Don't Know* Posters, 11" x 17" Elementary SPANISH	$40.00		
		TOTAL $	

TITLE	Price	QTY	TOTAL $
Academic Language Cards and Activity Booklet, ENGLISH	$19.95		
Academic Language Cards, SPANISH	$9.95		
		TOTAL $	

TITLE	Price	QTY	TOTAL $
Please Speak In Complete Sentences Poster 24" x 36" ☐ ENGLISH ☐ SPANISH	$9.95		
20 pack *Please Speak In Complete Sentences* Posters, 11" x 17" ☐ ENGLISH ☐ SPANISH	$40.00		
		TOTAL $	

SHIPPING 9% of order total, minimum $14.95
5-7 business days to ship.
If needed sooner please call for rates.

TAX EXEMPT? please fax a copy of your certificate along with order.

GRAND TOTAL	$
DISCOUNT	$
SHIPPING	$
TAX	$
FINAL TOTAL	$

NAME

SHIPPING ADDRESS   CITY   STATE, ZIP

PHONE NUMBER   EMAIL ADDRESS

TO ORDER BY FAX
to **(949) 200-4384**
please complete
credit card info *or*
attach purchase order

☐ Visa ☐ MasterCard ☐ Discover ☐ AMEX

CARD #   EXPIRES
                                mm/yyyy
SIGNATURE   CVV

☐ **Purchase Order**

please make
P.O. out to
Seidlitz Education